Praise for 99 Red Ball[...]

"One-hit wonders are as important to a c[...] standing of American popular music as ar[...] or The Beatles. Kudos to Brent Mann for telling their stories with wit, attitude and affection. Like many of the 'wonders' he writes about, I give it a ten. It's got a good beat and you can dance to it." —PETE FORNATALE, MIXEDBAGRADIO.COM

"Now I know why you wrote the book, Brent. You had to get that plethora of facts out of your head before it exploded! What better place to store them than between the covers of a book called *99 Red Balloons*. Prepare to be amazed and stupefied to find out that Katrina Leskanich ('Walking on Sunshine' by Katrina & the Waves) was the most honest of all the one-shot artists: 'I'm just an American girl trying to make a buck.' And did you know that Dave Loggins ('Please Come to Boston') is Kenny Loggins's cousin? Hey, I love 'em. They kept me on the radio for a long time." —DR. DON ROSE, DRDONROSE.COM

"Very interesting reading. Nice blend of music history and obscure facts." —PAT UPTON, LEAD SINGER OF THE SPIRAL STARECASE, "MORE TODAY THAN YESTERDAY" (ONE-HIT WONDER #20)

"Totally fun reading! And, from my point of view, a much appreciated survey written by an obviously incorrigible pop/rock fanatic." —STEVE FORBERT, "ROMEO'S TUNE" (ONE-HIT WONDER #36), STEVEFORBERT.COM

"*99 Red Balloons* spotlights all the timeless one-hit songs that have provided the soundtrack for our lives. Brent Mann has written a fun book about these classic tunes that will live forever." —BERTIE HIGGINS, "KEY LARGO" (ONE-HIT WONDER #75), BERTIEHIGGINS.COM

"I've just been reading Brent Mann's manuscript of his book *99 Red Balloons.* It's been a trip through time for me. I remember most every song and artist mentioned in the book, and many of the songs are on my favorite all-time list as well. It brought back a flood of great memories. I thought Brent's assessment of The Sanford/Townsend Band's plight was astute. I'm not sure we would have attained the stature of The Doobie Brothers, but I've always felt that had the timing been different we would have left a larger mark on the music scene. It's a great read for any music buff, and I highly recommend Brent Mann's *99 Red Balloons.*" —JOHN TOWNSEND, THE SANFORD/TOWNSEND BAND, "SMOKE FROM A DISTANT FIRE" (ONE-HIT WONDER #8), JOHNTOWN.COM

"Brent's passion for music is infectious, and his research and knowledge is downright impressive! The more I read *99 Red Balloons,* the more I wanted to know, and I realized how little I actually knew about these great songs that have defined benchmarks in our lives."

—STEPHANIE MELVILLE, THE BREEZE RADIO, NEW ZEALAND

"This is a long-overdue book about one-hit wonders that has a 'can't put it down' quality because each page is filled with incredibly interesting tidbits of information about the artist and song that keep the reader turning the page. The research alone would have sent most people into therapy. Brent Mann is obviously a huge fan of music and the people who make it. 'Into the Night' is hanging in the Rock and Roll Hall of Fame, but this book will be on my coffee table for any and all to read."

—BENNY MARDONES, "INTO THE NIGHT" (ONE-HIT WONDER #3), BENNYMARDONES.COM

99 Red Balloons...
and 100 Other All-Time Great One-Hit Wonders

BRENT MANN

CITADEL PRESS
Kensington Publishing Corp.
www.kensingtonbooks.com

CITADEL PRESS BOOKS are published by

Kensington Publishing Corp.
850 Third Avenue
New York, NY 10022

Copyright © 2003 Brent Mann

All Kensington titles, imprints, and distributed lines are available at special quantity discounts for bulk purchases for sales promotions, premiums, fund-raising, educational, or institutional use. Special book excerpts or customized printings can also be created to fit specific needs. For details, write or phone the office of the Kensington special sales manager: Kensington Publishing Corp., 850 Third Avenue, New York, NY 10022, attn: Special Sales Department; phone 1-800-221-2647.

CITADEL PRESS and the Citadel logo are Reg. U.S. Pat. & TM off.

First printing: November 2003
10 9 8 7 6 5 4 3 2 1
Printed in the United States of America

Library of Congress Control Number: 2003101245
ISBN 0-8065-2516-9

This book is dedicated with love and gratitude
to my mother, Tanny McCarthy Mann.

Contents

Acknowledgments

I'd like to thank Richard Ember, my superb editor, for all his excellent efforts on my behalf. Thanks also to Bruce Bender, the managing director of Citadel Press. In addition, a heartfelt thank-you to my wonderful literary agents, Frank Scatoni and Greg Dinkin of Venture Literary. I also want to thank Citadel's art director, Kristine Noble.

A heartfelt thank-you also to Stephanie Melville, Dr. Don Rose, Bertie Higgins, Steve Forbert, Therese Boyd, Pete Fornatale, John Townsend, John Rhys Eddins, Casey Kasem, Benny Mardones, Pat Upton, and Ben McLane.

Thanks must also go to the following people for their love, friendship, and encouragement during the writing of *99 Red Balloons:* Tanny McCarthy Mann, Dennis Coates, Kyle Mann, Leslie Doyle, JT Mann, Ann Mann, Veronica Mann, Tyler Mann, Rebecca Queeney, Tom Queeney, Gary Tsyporin, Diane Tsyporin, Jeremy Tsyporin, Kevin Wilk, Michael Levine, Alyson Boxman Levine, Steve Begley, Lynn Guberman, Pete Fogel, Shari Kamburoff, Lisa Cronin, Ellen Lynch, Joyce Harrington, Telly Davidson, Cory Cooper, and Pete Fornatale, Jr.

Introduction

The term "one-hit wonder" has, unfortunately, always been freighted with a rather negative connotation. It's easy to dismiss one-hit artists as either flash-in-the-pan has-beens or disposable, kitschy curiosities. Admittedly, one-hit wonderdom has produced its share of acts that are best forgotten—however, for every Toni Basil ("Mickey"), there is a Marc Cohn ("Walking in Memphis"). You bring up Sisqo and his silly "Thong Song," I'll counter with Oleta Adams and her beautiful "Get Here."

While the likes of, say, Michael Sembello ("Maniac"), Sir Mix-a-Lot ("Baby Got Back"), Baha Men ("Who Let the Dogs Out"), and Rick Dees & His Cast of Idiots ("Disco Duck") are undoubtedly fun one-hitters, those sorts of performers and their songs are definitely *not* what you'll find spotlighted here in the pages of *99 Red Balloons*. No, I'm taking you on a musical tour that focuses on the Doris Troys ("Just One Look"), Steve Forberts ("Romeo's Tune"), and Marshall Crenshaws ("Someday, Someway")—the all-time classic one-hit wonders. Excellent songs from fascinating people.

By the way, while the vast majority of the 101 artists featured on our survey scored only one Top 40 single, a few (*e.g.*, a-ha, Looking Glass, and Spandau Ballet) did chart multiple times. However, in spirit, all the acts highlighted are very much one-hit wonders, even if they landed two or three songs on the Top 40. Let's use Looking Glass as an example. In the summer of 1972, the band reached #1 with "Brandy (You're a Fine Girl)," a smash that stayed on the charts for 14 weeks. Then, a year later, Looking Glass dented the Top 40 again, this time with a record called "Jimmy Loves Mary-Anne," which stalled at #33 and fell off the charts after only three weeks.

So, the question becomes: Is Looking Glass a one-hit wonder? I say, yes—absolutely! I mean, let's be honest, "Jimmy Loves Mary-Anne" *peaked* at #33, and back in the early 70s, really only about 15 songs were in a Top 40 station's regular rotation at any given time, so a single that limped to #33 and disappeared after less than a month can hardly be called a hit. Looking Glass is remembered today for one tune and one tune only: "Brandy."

I know that I'll never see my name anywhere near the Top 40 pop charts, so I stand in genuine awe of the musical talent of every singer, musician, and songwriter I've had the privilege of writing about in *99 Red Balloons*. These incredible performers have brought me count-less hours of pleasure. I hope you enjoy your tour of the 101 all-time best one-hit wonders.

New York City

#101

"Walking on Sunshine"
by Katrina & the Waves, 1985

I feel alive, I feel a love
I feel a love that's really real

Peaked nationally at #9
Lead singer: Katrina Leskanich
Written by Kimberley Rew

"This is a weird and wonderful group," says Katrina
[Leskanich]. "We're four very different people, and sometimes the teacups fly. Kim's your typical eccentric Ray
Davies type; I'm just an American girl trying to make a
buck."
                    —*RECORD COLLECTOR* MAGAZINE, NOVEMBER 1997

Although their lead vocalist, Katrina Leskanich, was a native of To-
peka, Kansas, Katrina & the Waves were based in London. During the
early to mid-80s, there must have been some potent, magical one-hit
wonder dust floating in the air above the U.K.'s capital, because from
1983 through 1986, the city straddling the River Thames produced a
seemingly endless parade of memorable, and sometimes quirky, one-
hit acts: After the Fire ("Der Kommissar"), Boys Don't Cry ("I Wanna
Be a Cowboy"), Kate Bush ("Running Up That Hill"), Haircut One Hundred ("Love Plus One"), Paul Hardcastle ("19"), Kajagoogoo ("Too
Shy"), and Re-Flex ("The Politics of Dancing"), as well as the first
stop on our tour of the 101 best one-hit wonders in pop music his-

tory, Katrina & the Waves, an outfit composed of Alex Cooper, Vince de la Cruz, Katrina Leskanich, and Kimberley Rew.

"Walking on Sunshine" spent more than three months in the Top 40, reaching as high as #9. Here was a song that charged out of the gate with bright, boundless energy, the sort of joyously manic track that could set any roomful of people, no matter how staid, to frenzied dancing in no time flat. Indeed, if there was ever any doubt about this tune's upbeat vibe, just consider the titles of some of the CD compilations "Walking on Sunshine" has appeared on in recent years: *Smash Hits—Party Mix, Greatest Sports Rock and Jams, Hi-Octane Hard Drivin' Hits!* and *Hot Summer Fun Party Music.* Katrina & the Waves' number was also heard on *Bean: The Album,* the soundtrack to *Bean,* the goofy, highly forgettable Rowan Atkinson film from 1997.

During their 14-year existence, from 1983 through 1997, the band issued nine albums, including two "best of" collections. "Walking on Sunshine," incidentally, is featured on no fewer than four of their nine LPs, which is perfectly in keeping with the old record industry adage: If you score a Top 10 hit, get as much mileage out of it as you can.

By the way, over the years, "Walking on Sunshine" has become a darling of the worldwide television advertising community. Americans will recall that the song was used on a TV spot for Claritin, an allergy medication. In England, JJB Sports employed the tune to sell its sporting goods on the telly. And viewers Down Under will remember "Walking on Sunshine" from adverts promoting tourism in Queensland, Australia.

Brent's Two Cents: In September of '85, a few months after "Walking on Sunshine" shot up the charts to #9, Katrina & the Waves' "Do You Want Crying" spent two weeks in the Top 40, peaking at #37. Then, in the summer of 1989, the band landed a #16 single called "That's the Way."

So, the group really shouldn't be considered one-hit wonders at all, right? Well, in a word: wrong. Katrina & the Waves are as much one-hitters as, say, Vicki Sue Robinson ("Turn the Beat Around") or Walter Egan ("Magnet and Steel"). There are certain instances, and this is a prime example, where an act with multiple Top 40 entries is *in spirit* very much a one-hit wonder. Hey, we're all friends here, so we can be honest with each other: none of us ever heard "That's the Way" or "Do You Want Crying" played on the radio. Katrina & the Waves: talented, to be sure, but a group that will forever be associated with just one song, "Walking on Sunshine."

#100

"How Bizarre" by OMC, 1997

Destination unknown
As we pull in for some gas

Peaked nationally at #4
Lead singer: Pauly Fuemana
Written by Alan Jansson and Pauly Fuemana

[Pauly] Fuemana grew up in a New Zealand ghetto called Otara, which is kind of like the South Bronx of Auckland. He describes it as the poorest section of the city, "where all the Polynesians were shipped." With little education or opportunity for escape, Fuemana was headed for a life of crime.
—MIKE ROSS, WRITING IN THE JULY 17, 1997, EDITION OF *EXPRESS*, A CANADIAN PUBLICATION

What Mike Ross wrote above is interesting because it's seldom that you see the words "New Zealand" and "ghetto" used in the same sentence. Auckland, however, like any city of 400,000, obviously has its share of impoverished neighborhoods, Otara being chief among them. It's ironic, then, that OMC, the one-hit subject at hand, is actually an abbreviation for Otara Millionaires Club.

As pop fans, what exactly do we know of Kiwi music? Well, the phrase "next to nothing" immediately springs to mind. Uh, let's see, weren't Men at Work from New Zealand? Nope, Australia. Wait! What about Split Enz? They were a Kiwi band, right? Actually, yes, they were. Tim Finn and his brother, Neil, the driving forces behind Split Enz, hailed from Auckland. Of course, the Finns later teamed up under the Crowded House banner, scoring Top 40 records with "Something So Strong" and "Don't Dream It's Over," the latter zooming all the way to #2 in 1987.

So, at least in terms of the American audience, pop/rock from New Zealand began and ended with Mr. and Mrs. Finn's progeny—that is, until the summer of '97, when an unusual track started airing on FM stations from Key West in Florida to Kodiak in Alaska. Here was an inscrutable tune that mentioned 1969 Chevrolets, acrobats, and helicopters. It was all very random and surreal, yet, at the same time, utterly refreshing. The song, aptly enough, was called "How Bizarre," by an outfit named OMC. OMC? Didn't they do "So in Love" and "If You Leave" back in the mid-80s? No, that was OMD—Orchestral Manoeuvres in the Dark, a British group.

OMC was assumed to be an actual, proper *band*, and, indeed, it did begin as such, but at the time of "How Bizarre," it was, for all intents and purposes, a solo project of the aforementioned Pauly Fuemana, an Aucklander of Maori and Polynesian descent.

Fuemana's Top 5 smash appeared on the 1997 CD *How Bizarre*, the first and only OMC album. The single spent an incredible 36 weeks in the Top 40, and, in fact, during 1997, no record was spun over the U.S. airwaves more times than "How Bizarre." In addition, the accompanying video became an MTV and VH-1 staple. Not surprisingly, OMC's release topped the charts in Fuemana's native New Zealand. It reached #1 in Canada, Ireland, and Australia, as well, while peaking at #5 in England. Today, however, outside of places like Tauranga, Wellington, Christchurch, and, naturally, Auckland, the Otara Millionaires Club is mostly a fading, late-90s memory, but also undeniably an all-time classic one-hit wonder.

#99

"Please Come to Boston" by Dave Loggins, 1974

I'm the number one fan
Of the man from Tennessee

Peaked nationally at #5
Lead singer: Dave Loggins
Written by Dave Loggins

I don't think that most people realize the debt that con-
temporary bands like Pavement and Hole owe to Dave
Loggins, who was out criss-crossing the USA playing
Indie Rock long before the term was coined.

—AMAZON.COM CUSTOMER REVIEW OF *PLEASE COME TO*
BOSTON, A DAVE LOGGINS GREATEST HITS CD
RELEASED IN 1995

First off, let's not confuse Dave Loggins with Kenny Loggins, his more
famous cousin. *Kenny* Loggins was the guy who hooked up with Jim
Messina in the early 70s to wax cool singles like "Thinking of You"
and "Your Mama Don't Dance." He also partnered with Stevie Nicks
in 1978 for the smash "Whenever I Call You 'Friend'." So, Loggins &
Messina; duet with Fleetwood Mac's Stevie Nicks: *that's* Kenny Loggins.

Now, the subject at hand, *Dave* Loggins, well, he never managed
to enjoy the chart success of ol' Cousin Kenny, but he did write and
record "Please Come to Boston," a lovely, heartfelt song, and a classic one-hit track that earned the singer from Tennessee a Grammy
nomination for Best Pop Vocal Performance.

The power of Loggins's lone Top 40 tune, which raced all the way
to #5 in the summer of '74, derived from the universal sentiment it

conveyed. Millions of listeners instantly connected with the record's message of longing for a faraway lover, and pleading with that person to join you in a distant city to start a new life together. "Please Come to Boston" expressed love, hope, and frustration—all deep human emotions.

Between 1972 and 1977, Dave Loggins issued four albums: *Personal Belongings, Apprentice (In a Musical Workshop), Country Suite,* and *One Way Ticket to Paradise.* "Please Come to Boston" appeared on 1974's *Apprentice (In a Musical Workshop),* which is still in print. Incidentally, the second cut on *Personal Belongings,* his debut LP, was "Pieces of April." While this song did not chart for Loggins, it did for Three Dog Night, peaking at #19 in late 1972.

By the way, "Please Come to Boston" has found its way onto many compilation compact discs over the years, including *Rock Artifacts, Vol. 2, 70's Greatest Rock Hits: High Times,* and *Billboard Top Soft Rock Hits: 1974.* The Loggins tune has also been covered by artists such as Joan Baez, David Allan Coe, Reba McEntire, and Willie Nelson.

In recent years, Dave Loggins has remained extremely active in the music business, mostly as a highly sought-after country song-writer. He's penned smashes for Toby Keith ("Pick 'Em Up and Lay 'Em Down"), Alabama ("40 Hour Week" and "She and I"), Wynonna Judd ("She Is His Only Need"), and Restless Heart ("Wheels" and "Fast Movin' Train").

"Please Come to Boston" put Beantown on the one-hit wonder map, but Boston is certainly not the only city with a one-hit connection. There's also "The City of New Orleans" by Arlo Guthrie, Paper Lace's "The Night Chicago Died," "Walking in Memphis" by Marc Cohn, "Next Plane to London" by The Rose Garden, and of course, The Ad Libs's "The Boy from New York City."

#98

"I'm Too Sexy"
by Right Said Fred (R*S*F), 1992

I'm too sexy for Milan, too sexy for Milan
New York and Japan

Peaked nationally at #1
Lead singer: Richard Fairbrass
Written by Fred Fairbrass, Richard Fairbrass, and Rob
    Manzoli

From total obscurity, the band [Right Said Fred] became
the darlings of 1992 with the release of their debut single, "I'm Too Sexy," and proved that bald men in tight
Lycra shorts can become the ultimate pop stars!

—RIGHTSAIDFRED.COM

"I Want to Hold Your Hand" was the first song released by The Beatles
in the United States, and it went all the way to #1 in early 1964,
spending seven weeks in the top spot. Amazingly, it took another 28
years before a second British band managed to land its American
debut at #1 for at least three weeks. The group was Right Said Fred,
aka R*S*F, a trio composed of brothers Fred and Richard Fairbrass
and Rob Manzoli, and the tune was "I'm Too Sexy."

"Kookie, Kookie (Lend Me Your Comb)" by Edd Byrnes, "Tie Me
Kangaroo Down, Sport" by Rolf Harris, Loudon Wainwright's "Dead
Skunk," and Bob & Doug McKenzie's "Take Off"—the Top 40 has wit-
nessed a long line of novelty one-hit wonder singles, and in 1992,
"I'm Too Sexy" joined the ranks.

Right Said Fred's track was a goofy, good-natured lampooning of
fashion models, workout freaks, and other assorted narcissists, the

kind of fabulously superficial creatures who never met a mirror they didn't like, all set to an infectious, pulsating dance beat. "I'm Too Sexy" initially appeared on a 1992 album simply called *Up*; however, the song's runaway worldwide success prompted the issuance of an immediate follow-up CD, *I'm Too Sexy*, which contained no fewer than seven distinct re-mixes of R*S*F's #1 smash, among them: "Betty's Mix," "Catwalk Mix," "Spanish Version," as well as the obligatory "Extended Club Mix." Can you say *overkill*?

By the way, the video for "I'm Too Sexy" fit the material exquisitely. There were the Brothers Fairbrass, bare-chested and dressed in black pants, cavorting among bikini-clad babes, all of whom were furiously snapping photos of Fred and Richard. Interspersed throughout the campy festivities was stock footage of runway models. Antonio Banderas would have been proud—too sexy, indeed!

Right Said Fred, minus original member Rob Manzoli, is still very much a going concern. In fact, in 2002, they released their fifth album, *Stand Up*, and while it's safe to say R*S*F won't be headlining at Manhattan's Beacon Theater or San Francisco's Warfield anytime soon, the lads still enjoy a loyal and enthusiastic following in their native England, as well as Germany.

You might remember hearing "I'm Too Sexy" in a television commercial for the Toyota Camry back in 2001. Over the years, numerous one-hit wonders have been used—throughout the world—to push everything from cars to soft drinks. For example, a Canadian TV spot for Diet Pepsi featured "I Ran (So Far Away)," A Flock of Seagulls' #9 record from 1982. Then, here in the States, there was Jaguar pressing Chris Isaak's "Wicked Game" into service to sell its X-Type series of automobiles. And if you lived in Tokyo, you might recall "Relax" by Frankie Goes to Hollywood being employed to hawk Lemoria, a refreshing, and one might surmise *relaxing*, lemon-flavored beverage.

#97

"Just One Look" by Doris Troy, 1963

Just one look and I fell so hard
In love with you, oooh-ooh, oooh-ooh

Peaked nationally at #10
Lead singer: Doris Troy
Written by Gregory Carroll and Doris Payne

> Of all the people in this city [Las Vegas] who had a con-
> nection to the late George Harrison, 20-year Las Vegas
> resident Doris Troy probably had the closest.
>
> —*LETTERS TO BUCK* COLUMN IN LASVEGASWEEKLY.COM

Her name at birth was Doris Higginson. When writing songs back in
the 60s, her *nom de plume* was Doris Payne, with Payne being the
surname of one of her grandmothers. But the name on her lone Top
40 single, "Just One Look," was Doris Troy.

Troy was born in New York City on January 6, 1937. Her father, the
Reverend Randolph Higginson, preached as a Baptist minister, which
may explain the joyous, yet grounded, gospel feel his daughter
brought to her #10 tune. If you listen closely, the thing that really
captures your ear about "Just One Look" is the immediacy and fresh-
ness of the record's sound—no fancy production tricks, no lushness
of a thousand and one strings, just some simple piano, bass, drums,
and Doris Troy's clear, soulful voice. You feel as though you're sitting
in a midtown Manhattan studio in 1963, the honored guest at a live
recording session. And hats off to Linda Ronstadt for her 1978 cover
of "Just One Look," as the Tucson, Arizona, native did a wonderfully
effective job of retaining the original's vibe, while at the same time
putting her own stamp on the track. By the way, The Hollies, the
English popsters recalled for hits like "Bus Stop," "On a Carousel,"

and "Carrie-Anne," waxed their own version of Troy's song back in '64, giving it a bright, British Invasion spin. Bryan Ferry of Roxy Music fame, the late Kirsty MacColl, as well as the pride of Springhill, Nova Scotia, Anne Murray, also covered "Just One Look." However, only Doris Troy's single managed to crack the charts.

That Troy never enjoyed the success of, say, a Dionne Warwick or a Diana Ross is perplexing. She certainly possessed the vocal ability, and she was definitely in the right place, New York City, to make it happen, but while Warwick, for example, can boast today of no fewer than 31 Top 40 records, starting with 1963's "Don't Make Me Over," Troy's total remains at just one. Why didn't the Pop Music Gods favor Doris Troy with her own Burt Bacharach and Hal David? Where was her Berry Gordy to lend a hand?

Of course, accumulating Top 40 hits as a solo act is not the only measure of a singer's career, and an inspection of Doris Troy's resume reveals her direct involvement in a wide variety of important musical projects, including providing backing vocals on legendary albums such as The Rolling Stones' *Let It Bleed* and Pink Floyd's *Dark Side of the Moon*. In addition, you can hear Troy's voice on classic tracks like "My Sweet Lord" by George Harrison and Carly Simon's "You're So Vain." What's more, in 1970, Apple Records issued an LP called *Doris Troy*, putting the songstress in the select company of Mary Hopkin, James Taylor, and Badfinger as among the few acts besides The Beatles to record on the Apple label.

Doris Troy is also the only one-hit wonder on our tour whose life inspired an Off-Broadway show, *Mama, I Want to Sing*. This musical, which premiered on March 23, 1983, at Manhattan's Heckscher Theatre and ran through the early 90s, holds the honor of being the highest-grossing Off-Broadway production ever. Then, in February of 1995, *Mama, I Want to Sing* opened in London's West End, with Chaka Khan, Deniece Williams, and Doris Troy in starring roles. Troy, incidentally, played the part of her own mother.

#96

"Break My Stride"
by Matthew Wilder, 1983

Last night I had the strangest dream
I sailed away to China in a little rowboat to find ya'

Peaked nationally at #5
Lead singer: Matthew Wilder
Written by Greg Prestopino and Matthew Wilder

The song ["Break My Stride"] was a gift to myself. I didn't
have the support of anyone in the business.
—MATTHEW WILDER, AS QUOTED IN *PEOPLE* MAGAZINE

The overall vibe of "Break My Stride" can be described in a single
word: "jaunty." Another good word might be "boppy." This is a high-
spirited ditty that bounces right along from start to finish, and in a
year that produced a raft of British one-hitters like Kajagoogoo ("Too
Shy"), After the Fire ("Der Kommissar"), and Thomas Dolby ("She
Blinded Me with Science"), it was refreshing to see that 1983 also
made room on the charts for an American artist such as Matthew
Wilder. By the way, Wilder did have another tune, "The Kid's American," that had a cup of coffee on the charts in early '84, peaking at a
faintly-on-the-radar #33; however, in spirit, the New York City native
must be considered a one-hit wonder.

Twenty years after its release, Wilder's Top 5 smash is still being
spun on Oldies and Lite-FM stations from Fresno to Philadelphia.
"Break My Stride" definitely possesses that rare musical quality known
as timelessness. Sure, the record was issued in 1983, but it easily
could have been a product of 1973 or even, for that matter, 2003. It's
simply a well-crafted piece of pop that has aged gracefully.

Matthew Wilder only waxed two albums: *I Don't Speak the Language* (1983) and *Bouncin' Off the Walls* (1984), with "Break My Stride" coming off his debut. Interestingly, in 1999, both LPs, which had been out of print, were re-packaged on the Collectables label as part of a double compact disc. Of course, Wilder's hit single has long been available on various compilation CDs, including *Feel Good Rock— Songs You Know by Heart,* where it shares space with three other classic one-hit tracks, "Rock On" (David Essex), "Hold Your Head Up" (Argent), and "Rock & Roll, Hoochie Koo" (Rick Derringer); *Back on My Feet Again*, an album that also highlights a tune called "Breakin' . . . There's No Stopping Us" by the obscure one-hit wonders known as Ollie & Jerry; and *Don't Touch My 45's: Great Lost Singles of the 80's,* which, in addition to "Break My Stride," features "When Your Heart Is Weak," a mostly forgotten but quite solid one-hitter from the summer of '85 by the band Cock Robin.

Even though Matthew Wilder has never managed to become a household name, he's still enjoyed an extremely successful career in the music business. Over the years, artists as diverse as Jimmy Cliff, Sheena Easton, Patti LaBelle, and Aaron Neville have all recorded songs penned by Wilder. In addition, he's produced best-selling CDs, most notably No Doubt's *Tragic Kingdom*, which spawned "Don't Speak," a #1 monster that spent a full year in the Top 40. Wilder also contributed music to the *Mulan* soundtrack, for which he earned an Academy Award nomination. So, this man who went from paying the bills by singing jingles for Honda car commercials to scoring a #5 record has done just fine for himself, never allowing anything to break his stride.

#95

"What's Up" by 4 Non Blondes, 1993

And I scream at the top of my lungs
What's going on?!

Peaked nationally at #14
Lead singer: Linda Perry
Written by Linda Perry

The money was great, the fame was addictive, but something else was missing from her life. She [Linda Perry]
walked out of the recording studio and away from 4 Non
Blondes, and the band fell apart.
—RACHEL PEPPER, WRITING IN *QSF* MAGAZINE

Song titles can be downright baffling sometimes. For example, 4 Non
Blondes' sole Top 40 record *should* have been called "What's Going
On." After all, lead singer Linda Perry belted out the refrain "What's
going on?!" no fewer than eight times throughout the course of the
record. Never once did she ask the musical question "What's up?"
Perhaps 4 Non Blondes wanted to avoid confusion with Marvin
Gaye's "What's Going On," a #2 smash in 1971. Or maybe the band
just simply decided to be cryptic. No matter what the reason, the
track was entitled "What's Up," and it spent a solid 17 weeks on the
charts in the spring and summer of 1993.

"The Sign" by Ace of Bass, Boyz II Men's "I'll Make Love to You,"
and "A Whole New World (Aladdin's Theme)" by Peabo Bryson and
Regina Belle—those were the sorts of wimpy tunes dominating the
FM landscape when "What's Up" rode into town to kick some Top 40
ass. With Linda Perry's batten-down-the-hatches lead vocals, as well
as her insistent strumming on acoustic guitar, 4 Non Blondes' record
was the musical equivalent of slamming down a double shot of Wild

Turkey in a fern bar packed with white wine drinkers. Of all the memorable one-hit wonder singles on our tour, two really stick out for their positive spirit, infectiousness, and uncontrollable exuberance: "You Get What You Give" by New Radicals and "What's Up."

4 Non Blondes released only one album, 1992's *Bigger, Better, Faster, More!*, on which "What's Up" was the third cut. The track was also found on compilation CDs such as *Born to Be Wild* and *Now That's What I Call Music 1993*. If you listen closely to all 11 songs on *Bigger, Better, Faster, More!*, it's plain that only "What's Up" had chart potential. The other offerings, while plenty energetic, lack the underlying playful smile found in the band's lone hit. A clear, booming voice like Perry's is a terrific gift, but it needs to be dialed-back on occasion for maximum effectiveness. For a pop/rock singer, less is often more.

While Linda Perry was indisputably the face of and driving force behind 4 Non Blondes, she was, in fact, very much part of a genuine group whose other members were Christa Hillhouse (bass), Dawn Richardson (drums), and Roger Rocha (lead guitar). And after *Bigger, Better, Faster, More!* sold more than five million copies, spawning a Top 15 smash, Hillhouse, Richardson, and Rocha were naturally eager to keep the momentum going, but Perry had *her* eyes on a solo career, so she called it quits, and today, San Francisco's 4 Non Blondes are remembered as classic one-hit wonders.

> Linda Perry has always been very open about the fact that she is gay. Here's what the singer had to say in a magazine called *Girlfriends*: "I've never not been outspoken about my sexuality. Everyone knew I was gay—I mean, I was on David Letterman with DYKE on my shirt!"

#94

"Tarzan Boy" by Baltimora, 1986

Jungle life, I'm far away from nowhere
On my own like Tarzan Boy

Peaked nationally at #13
Lead singer: Baltimora
Written by Naimy Hackett and Maurizio Bassi

Baltimora was the name adopted by Northern Ireland's Jimmy McShane, a talented performer who died of AIDS on March 28, 1995, at the age of 37, but not before leaving behind a terrific one-hit wonder called "Tarzan Boy."

Of all the 101 songs on our tour of the most memorable one-hitters, "Tarzan Boy" is perhaps the strangest, and, yet, at the same time, it's also probably the simplest. It tells the story of a young man who is living alone in the jungle, leading a life of complete freedom away from the civilized world. And this free spirit, this Tarzan Boy, is trying to persuade a friend to join him in his wild, primitive existence.

The feeling that pervades Baltimora's single is one of exhilarating escape, fleeing the mundane for the exotic. And with its pulsating techno beat, "Tarzan Boy" is among the best dance tracks ever. Just consider the titles of some of the compilation CDs the tune has been a part of: *80s Dance Party, Vol. 3, The Best 80s Non-Stop Party Album*, and *Dancemania Super Classics, Vol. 3*. "Tarzan Boy" also appears on the soundtrack to *Beverly Hills Ninja*, the 1997 Chris Farley movie. It's on the *Teenage Mutant Ninja Turtles III* soundtrack, as well. The reasons behind this affinity the producers of ninja-related flicks have had for Baltimora's Top 20 hit are not entirely clear. By the way, in 1993, "Tarzan Boy" was used in a television spot for Cool Mint Listerine. The ad was built around a bottle of refreshing mouthwash swinging from vine to vine deep within the consumer jungle. In fact, it's a fair bet that more people know the track as "The Listerine Song" than by its real title.

For a tune that always conjured up such vivid mental imagery, it was only natural that "Tarzan Boy" also translated into an unforgettable video, a mid-80s MTV staple. There was Baltimora, clad in casual white pants and a totally unbuttoned brown shirt, underneath which he wore a leopard-skin sash. In the shadows to the singer's right and left were small palm trees. As Baltimora sang and danced his way through the number, the background, which depicted what looked like a crude jungle village, changed color constantly. The overall effect was to put the viewer in a mood of dark, mysterious fun and adventure. The video fit the material perfectly.

During his 37 years, Jimmy McShane only released two albums: *Baltimora* and *Living in the Background*, "Tarzan Boy" coming off the latter. Neither of his LPs remains in print. And, if not for his lone Top 40 record, the man from Londonderry would be completely forgotten. We'll give the last word on Baltimora to a woman named Dawn Marie, a commentator on 80s music for the about.com website: "No one remembers the name of the song, and certainly not Jimmy [McShane], however, his song 'Tarzan Boy' is to this day one of the most beloved 80s pop songs."

> In addition to Baltimora, the Irish have given the music world some of the most diverse and fascinating one-hit wonders of the last 30 years, including Sinead O'Connor ("Nothing Compares 2 U"), Enya ("Orinoco Flow [Sail Away]"), and Thin Lizzy ("The Boys Are Back in Town").

#93

"Driver's Seat"
by Sniff 'n' the Tears, 1979

Jenny was sweet
She'd always smile for the people she'd meet

Peaked nationally at #15
Lead singer: Paul Roberts
Written by Paul Roberts

First of all, major points to this London-based band for having what has to be considered among the coolest, most creative monikers ever: Sniff 'n' the Tears.

The group was composed of Chris Birkin, Mick Dyche, Alan Feald-man, Loz Netto, Paul Roberts, and Luigi Salvoni, and although you'd be hard pressed to find anyone who owns a Sniff 'n' the Tears album, they're still remembered by millions for waxing "Driver's Seat," a classic one-hitter.

A fellow named Tony Parsons, writing in the November 11, 1978, edition of *New Music Express*, called Sniff 'n' the Tears' lone Top 40 record "that rare breed—dance music that isn't disco." That's the perfect description of "Driver's Seat," a spot-on characterization of the single's sound: *dance music that isn't disco.* During 1979, a year when the airwaves were heavy with the pulsating energy of "Ring My Bell" by Anita Ward, Donna Summer's "Hot Stuff" and "Bad Girls," as well as "I Will Survive" by Gloria Gaynor, "Driver's Seat" blended right in. However, as Tony Parsons correctly pointed out, unlike Mlles. Ward, Summer, and Gaynor, Sniff 'n' the Tears were not purveying disco, but rather an unusual mix of straight-ahead rock 'n' roll and early New Wave, all with a highly danceable beat. Indeed, in retro-spect, the most fascinating thing about "Driver's Seat" is how it was among a handful of British one-hitters from late 1979 that was exposing the mainstream pop/rock audience to so-called New Wave for the first time. Records like "Cruel to Be Kind" by Nick Lowe, "Hold On" by Ian Gomm, and especially "Pop Muzik" by M were foretelling the arrival of a decade of Thompson Twins, Pet Shop Boys, and Simple Minds. Obviously, songs like "Cruel to Be Kind" and "Driver's Seat" were not drenched in a 1984 vibe like, say, the Thompson Twins' "Doctor! Doctor!" or "Hold Me Now," but New Wave seeds were definitely being planted in the summer and fall of '79, no doubt about it.

During Sniff 'n' the Tears' relatively brief existence, 1978 through 1982, the outfit released four albums: *Fickle Heart, The Game's Up, Love Action,* and *Ride Blue Divide,* with their #15 hit coming off their debut. "Driver's Seat" also appears on Volume 2 of the *Boogie Nights* soundtrack. In addition, the tune can be found on *Good Clean Fun: The Chiswick Sampler* (Chiswick being Sniff 'n' the Tears' first record label) and *Sounds of the Seventies: AM Heavy Hits.*

Perhaps more than any other year, 1979 yielded the widest variety of one-hit wonders. The musical styles were all over the map in '79. You had disco tracks like "Got to Be Real" (Cheryl Lynn), "Knock on Wood" (Amii Stewart), "Ring My Bell" (Anita Ward), and "Born to Be Alive" (Patrick Hernandez) bumping into early New Wave records like "Pop Muzik" (M). Then there was an instrumental like "Music Box Dancer" (Frank Mills) sharing the airwaves with the jazzy pop soul of "What You Won't Do for Love" (Bobby Caldwell). Of course, 1979 also spawned a raft of sappy one-hitters such as "Just When I Needed You Most" (Randy Van Warmer), "You Take My Breath Away" (Rex Smith), and "You're Only Lonely" (J.D. Souther).

#92

"One of Us" by Joan Osborne, 1995

What if God was one of us
Just a slob like one of us

Peaked nationally at #4
Lead singer: Joan Osborne
Written by Eric Bazilian

To me, the beauty of "One of Us" is its ability to make
people think about God without filtering their thoughts
through the structure of organized religion.

—JOAN OSBORNE, AMERICA ONLINE/VH-1 CHAT
TRANSCRIPT, NOVEMBER 30, 1995

Remember a one-hitter from 1971 called "One Toke Over the Line" by
Brewer & Shipley? Now, we could slap *Led Zeppelin IV* on the old
turntable, pass around a bottle of Boone's Farm Strawberry, and
spend hours discussing the deep meaning of this tune, but to save
time, not to mention a pounding hangover, let's just say Brewer &
Shipley's ditty was essentially about some dude who was high waiting for his train to arrive. Likewise, concerning the subject at hand,
"One of Us" by Joan Osborne, we could parse this one-hit wonder
over a bottomless cup of hazelnut decaf, searching for subtle hints to
its cosmic significance, but, again, let's cut to the chase: "One of Us,"
a track that spent five months in the Top 40, peaking at #4, basically
challenged listeners to imagine a world where "The Supreme Being"
was just a regular guy, an everyday working stiff, living anonymously
among us.

Granted, it was an extremely odd premise for a pop single; however, its commercial success demonstrated that a mid-90s audience
was willing to embrace, or at least *consider,* a song outside of the

standard Celine Dion and Mariah Carey treacle. And it's interesting to note how it's often been classic one-hitters like "One of Us," "Get a Job" (The Silhouettes), "You Get What You Give" (New Radicals), "Beds Are Burning" (Midnight Oil), and "Signs" (Five Man Electrical Band)—records with a social bite and a philosophical point of view—that have provided some much-needed spice to the pop charts.

"One of Us" was culled from *Relish,* Joan Osborne's sophomore album. Her first LP, 1991's *Soul Show,* displayed promise, but it wasn't until the release of *Relish* in 1995 that the Kentucky native enjoyed a spot in the Top 40. Curiously, her third effort, *Righteous Love,* wasn't on shelves until 2000, by which time the momentum created by "One of Us" had fully dissipated. In 2002, Osborne issued *How Sweet It Is,* a CD notable only for its inclusion of "The Weight," the Robbie Robertson–penned gem from the 60s.

Today, Joan Osborne maintains an active touring schedule, playing venues like The Chance in Poughkeepsie, New York; San Francisco's Bimbo's 365 Club; and House of Blues in Lake Buena Vista, Florida.

Brent's Two Cents: When a Top 5 smash comes right out and refers to God as a "slob," it's only natural that the song and the artist will draw criticism from various religious quarters. Here's what The Catholic League had to say about "One of Us" and Joan Osborne: "If her admirers see something of the sacrilegious in her work, it is hard to maintain that Osborne doesn't have an agenda. It is our hope that she doesn't let her sentiments regarding Catholicism get in the way of whatever artistic abilities she has." By the way, if you read this Catholic League quote in your best Dana Carvey "Church Lady" voice, you get the full effect.

#91

"Sea Cruise" by Frankie Ford, 1959

So be my guest, you got nothing to lose
Won't you let me take you on a sea cruise

Peaked nationally at #14
Lead singer: Frankie Ford
Written by Huey Smith and Frankie Ford

Ford resents the term "one-hit wonder," and rightly
pointed out that his four recordings of "Sea Cruise" have
now sold over 30 million copies worldwide.
                              —ENCYCLOPEDIA OF POPULAR MUSIC

The name on his lone Top 40 single was Frankie Ford. The name on
his Louisiana birth certificate was Francis Guzzo. But no matter what
name he used—Ford or Guzzo—the singer waxed an all-time classic
one-hitter in "Sea Cruise," a song that still remains on the pop music
radar nearly 45 years after its release.

"Sea Cruise" was a combination of New Orleans R&B, boogie
woogie piano, old-fashioned rock 'n' roll, and even a dash of Dixie-
land jazz. With its driving bass, swinging saxophone, burn-the-house-
down piano, and of course, Ford's spirited, impassioned vocals, the
track was nothing short of a two-minute-and-forty-four-second
party—the kind of record that rocked, bopped, and swung from the
word "go."

Interestingly, back in '59, when "Sea Cruise" was first pressed on a
45 by Ace Records, it was the B-side to a tune called "Roberta."
Chartwise, the A-side went nowhere, while the flip-side zoomed to
#14. That same year, 1959, the Ace label also issued *Let's Take a Sea
Cruise with Frankie Ford,* a full-length album. This LP had long been
out of print until Edsel Records UK re-released it in 1999.

When "Sea Cruise" broke onto the national charts, the crooner and pianist from the Bayou State was only 19 years old, and it appeared as though a string of hits was likely. Things just didn't shake out that way, though. Solid as they were, follow-up singles such as "Alimony," "I Want to Be Your Man," and "Saturday Night Fish Fry" never dented the Top 40. A hitch in the Army during the early 1960s certainly didn't help Ford keep his career momentum going, either.

Now approaching the age of 65, Frankie Ford still resides in his hometown of Gretna, Louisiana, just outside of The Big Easy. And even though it's been more than four decades since "Sea Cruise" shared the AM airwaves with tunes like "Stagger Lee" by Lloyd Price and The Fleetwoods' "Come Softly to Me," the man who's earned the nickname "The New Orleans Dynamo" continues to entertain audiences from the Westbury Music Fair on Long Island to the legendary Surf Ballroom (the site of Buddy Holly's last performance) in Clear Lake, Iowa, to Rhythm Riot in Surrey, England.

February 3, 1959, was a Tuesday, and it was very early on the morning of the third that Buddy Holly, Ritchie Valens, and J.P. "The Big Bopper" Richardson died in a plane crash, mere hours after the trio of pioneering rock 'n' rollers had done a show at the aforementioned Surf Ballroom. February 3, 1959, of course, has become known as "The Day the Music Died."

Musically, though, the final year of the 50s did generate some bright spots, especially from one-hitters: Phil Phillips, who, like Frankie Ford, was a native Louisianan, reached #2 with "Sea of Love," while Bo Diddley scored his only chart single with a #20 song called "Say Man."

#90

"In a Big Country"
by Big Country, 1983

In a big country dreams stay with you
Like a lover's voice fires the mountainside

Peaked nationally at #17
Lead singer: Stuart Adamson
Written by Stuart Adamson, Mark Brzezicki, Tony Butler,
    and Bruce Watson

> The band [Big Country] were once touted as contenders
> with U2 for the "Celtic Rock" crown before the Irish band
> [U2] achieved stratospheric stardom.
> —JEEVAN VASAGAR, WRITING IN *THE GUARDIAN* NEWSPAPER

The 1983 nominees for the Best New Artist Grammy were Big Country, Culture Club, The Eurythmics, Men Without Hats, and Musical Youth. The winner, on the strength of monster singles like "Karma Chameleon," "Church of the Poison Mind," and "Do You Really Want to Hurt Me," was, of course, Boy George and his Culture Club. What's particularly interesting, though, was that three of the five Best New Artist contenders from '83 turned out to be memorable one-hit wonders: Musical Youth for a silly ditty called "Pass the Dutchie," Men Without Hats for an even sillier "The Safety Dance," and the subject at hand, Big Country, for their #17 record, "In a Big Country."

Big Country hailed from Dunfermline, Scotland, although the sound on their lone hit was straight out of County Donegal; so much so, in fact, that millions of American listeners assumed the outfit was Irish. But they were Scottish through and through, the same as fellow one-hitters Danny Wilson ("Mary's Prayer") and The Proclaimers ("I'm

Gonna Be [500 Miles]"). Incidentally, to the surprise of many, the Bay City Rollers, the mid-70s teen idols from Edinburgh best recalled for their tune "Saturday Night," were *not* one-hit wonders—indeed, between 1975 and 1977, the tartan-clad heartthrobs landed no fewer than six songs on the Top 40.

Because Big Country came to prominence around the same period as acts like The Human League, Thomas Dolby, Duran Duran, and The Motels, the Scotsmen were immediately dubbed New Wave, which was not exactly a proper categorization of the band's style. A more accurate description would have been "power Celtic folk," if such a label even exists. And this goes a long way toward explaining Big Country's status as one-hitters: Let's face it, after KYUU, WNBC, and WROR spin "Come on Eileen" and "In a Big Country" a few thousand times, it's not easy to break *another* power Celtic folk single, no matter how catchy it may be. The mainstream audience quickly gets its fill of a certain sound and then moves on to the *next* thing, and that's how one-hit wonders come to pass.

The lead vocalist for Big Country was Stuart Adamson, a man who, at the age of 43, took his own life in a Honolulu hotel room in December of 2001. It was a tragic ending for a singer who, during the early to mid-80s, had been on top of the music world, performing at Wembley Stadium as part of Live Aid; appearing on *Saturday Night Live*; and fronting a group whose debut album, *The Crossing,* had sold more than three million copies and spawned an unforgettable Top 20 song and classic one-hitter.

Brent's Two Cents: In researching this entry, I naturally went to Big Country's official website (bigcountry.co.uk), where I was struck by the following post to a forum concerning the group's legacy. I think what this anonymous fan wrote specifically about Big Country applies to many of the one-hit wonders featured in *99 Red Balloons*: "In my opinion, Big Country were one of the most successful bands ever. They made awesome music, with people they loved, connected deeply with a loyal fan base, and continued to create through a lot of adversity. If that isn't success, I don't know what is. We need to remember that achievement isn't really measured by chart position."

#89

"Closing Time" by Semisonic, 1998

So gather up your jackets and move it to the exits
I hope you have found a friend

Peaked nationally at #11
Lead singer: Dan Wilson
Written by Dan Wilson

Nobody's Ugly After 2 a.m.
—BUMPER STICKER

Every year a Grammy is presented in the category of Best Rock Song. Train's "Drops of Jupiter" snagged the honor in 2002. The year before that, it was "With Arms Wide Open" by Creed. At the 1999 Grammy Awards, the one-hit single at hand, "Closing Time" by Semisonic, nearly won Best Rock Song, but was edged out by Alanis Morissette's "Uninvited."

Semisonic is a three-man outfit based out of Minneapolis, the same city that gave us Prince, Morris Day, The Trashmen, and The Andrews Sisters, not to mention one-hitters Lipps, Inc., of "Funkytown" fame. The group, composed of John Munson, Jacob Slichter, and Dan Wilson, formed in 1995, and to date has issued four albums: *Pleasure, Great Divide, Feeling Strangely Fine,* and *All About Chemistry.* Their lone Top 40 hit came off 1998's *Feeling Strangely Fine.*

"Closing Time" spent a robust 29 weeks on the charts, peaking at #11. This tune, all piano and guitar, resonated so well with listeners, especially those in their 20s, because it dealt with a slice of life mil-

> Asked why his city [Minneapolis] is turning out so
> much music these days, the singer-guitarist [Bob
> Mould of Husker Du] quipped, "It's so cold in
> Minneapolis, you have to do something to keep
> warm."
>   —Craig Lee, writing in the *Los Angeles Times*
>   about the band Husker Du, December 15, 1984
>
> Minnesota is hardly synonymous with pop/rock music;
> however, consider the famous acts who have sprung from
> the Land of 10,000 Lakes: Husker Du (in both Danish and
> Norwegian, "Husker du?" means "Do you remember?"),
> Bob Dylan ("Positively 4th Street" and "Knockin' on
> Heaven's Door"), The Replacements, The Time ("Jerk-Out"
> and "Jungle Love"), Prince ("Purple Rain" and "Little Red
> Corvette"), Soul Asylum ("Runaway Train"), and Bobby Vee
> ("Take Good Care of My Baby" and "The Night Has a
> Thousand Eyes").

lions could relate to: being at a bar or club and trying to hook up with a member of the opposite sex as "last call" loomed. The Twin Cities trio had managed to wax the ultimate 1990s nobody-wants-to-go-home-alone record.

Why hasn't Semisonic enjoyed more success producing chart singles? Well, that's always been the $64,000 question regarding one-hit wonders, and *usually* there's no easy answer. However, in Semisonic's case, the root of the band's Top 40 shortcomings can be clearly pinpointed, namely, Dan Wilson's voice. The singer just doesn't possess the necessary pop/rock vocal chops. The songwriting talent is there. The musicianship is superb. But Wilson's voice is just too thin to carry off the material.

Although Semisonic is still together, their bassist, John Munson, has also found time to join forces with a guitarist named Matt Wilson (brother of Dan Wilson) in a duo called The Flops. According to The Flops' own website: "They are two men who have grown used to a life of rambling and horn-dogging from state to state. This new grouping is an attempt by John and Matt to maintain the lifestyle they have known." The phrase "horn-dogging from state to state"—has there ever been a more colorful description of the stereotypical rock 'n' roll lifestyle?

#88

"All the Young Dudes" by Mott the Hoople, 1972

*And my brother's back at home with his Beatles and
    his Stones
We never got it off on that revolution stuff*

Peaked nationally at #37
Lead singer: Ian Hunter
Written by David Bowie

Yes, David Bowie penned "All the Young Dudes," and, of course, Ziggy Stardust can certainly be heard singing backup on the track, but the classic one-hitter was definitely *not* a David Bowie single. No, this version of "All the Young Dudes," a song millions of transistor-toting teens were bopping to in the fall of '72, was the product of Mott the Hoople, the core members of which were Ian Hunter, Dale Griffin, Mick Ralphs, and Pete Watts.

First off, let's get the skinny on this group's highly unusual moniker. Who was Mott? And what, exactly, is a "hoople"? Well, a hoople is a tramp, a vagabond. As for Mott, that would be one Norman Mott, the protagonist of Willard Manus's 1960s comic novel, aptly titled *Mott the Hoople*. Apparently, the guys in the band were fond of Manus's writing, or, at least, they thought the name of his book possessed a certain ring, so these Englishmen from Hereford became known as Mott the Hoople.

For nearly 35 years, rock 'n' roll fans have been debating the meaning of "All the Young Dudes." Just what *is* this tune about, anyway? At one level, it plainly concerns itself with restless, disaffected youths, "dudes" who are bored with a working-class existence—a life of staying home, watching television, and listening to the same tired old Beatles and Rolling Stones records. On another level, however, "All the Young Dudes" is clearly about homosexual hustlers, randy street-corner rent boys looking for some action.

That Mott the Hoople's signature song contained gay undertones actually made perfect sense. The outfit was in the vanguard of the so-called glam rock movement, which spawned the likes of T. Rex, Gary Glitter, The New York Dolls, and of course, David Bowie, all of whom brought an undeniable same-sex sensibility to their work. Speaking of Bowie, not only did he offer "All the Young Dudes" to Mott the Hoople, which they obviously accepted, but the Thin White Duke also brought his "Suffragette City" to the band, which they rejected.

For a one-hit wonder, and a group that had a modest run from 1969 through 1976, it's amazing that some 20 Mott the Hoople albums, including "greatest hits" compilations, are still available, among them *All the Young Dudes*, the 1972 album that put the band on the Top 40 map.

Brent's Two Cents: I always thought Mott the Hoople was a *two*-hit wonder: in addition to "All the Young Dudes," surely their "All the Way from Memphis" also cracked the charts, right? Wrong. "Memphis" never dented the Top 40, which surprised me, as I remember hearing this song on the radio regularly back in the 70s. Never charted, though. Even in the world of pop and rock, sometimes the perception is very different from the reality. Of course, the best example of perception versus reality is the group Squeeze. Think of all the well-known singles these London-based New Wavers issued in the late 70s and early 80s, memorable tracks like "Tempted," "Black Coffee in Bed," "Take Me, I'm Yours," "Pulling Mussels (From the Shell)," and "Annie Get Your Gun." None of these landed on the Top 40. However, "Hourglass" and "853–5937," a pair of relatively obscure Squeeze cuts, *did* chart, at #15 and #32, respectively.

#87

"Beds Are Burning" by Midnight Oil, 1988

How can we dance when our Earth is turning
How can we sleep while our beds are burning

Peaked nationally at #17
Lead singer: Peter Garrett
Written by Peter Garrett, Rob Hirst, and Jim Moginie

Like fellow one-hit wonders the Divinyls, Midnight Oil hailed from Australia, but while the former was singing about lustful longing and masturbation in their #4 smash "I Touch Myself" from 1991, the latter was championing the rights of Aborigines in "Beds Are Burning."

Midnight Oil came together in 1975 in Sydney. Thirteen years later, at the time of their lone hit single, the outfit's line-up was Peter Garrett on lead vocals, Peter Gifford on bass, Rob Hirst on drums, Jim Moginie on keyboard, and Martin Rotsey on lead guitar.

"Beds Are Burning" could best be described as agit-pop, a song of protest, and the message was plain: The indigenous peoples of Australia, the so-called Abos, have been getting a raw deal forever, and now it's time to rectify the situation by paying reparations and giving them back their land. Heavy stuff for a Top 40 single. Of course, all the average American listener heard was a funky dance beat and some snazzy trombone work straight out of Henry Mancini's "Peter Gunn." Aboriginal land rights? It's safe to say that that particular theme might have been lost on at least a portion of the FM audience.

Midnight Oil's politically charged "Beds Are Burning" was the lead cut on the album *Diesel and Dust*. It later appeared on *20,000 Watt R.S.L.,* the band's greatest hits collection that was issued in 1997. In addition, two interesting covers of "Beds" were waxed in the 90s, one by Paul Shaffer, David Letterman's bandleader; the other by Split Lip, a group from Indiana. Shaffer's version came off a 1993 CD, *The World's Most Dangerous Party,* while Split Lip's, well, it was part of a compact disc called *Songs You May or May Not Have Heard Before,* which is indisputably among the funniest, most inventive album titles of all time.

For a country of only 20 million people, Australia has produced an unusually large number of acts that have enjoyed success on the American pop charts. Midnight Oil, Divinyls, Air Supply, Kylie Minogue, Little River Band, Rolf Harris, Olivia Newton-John, Men at Work, Helen Reddy, Tina Arena, AC/DC, Rick Springfield, INXS, the Bee Gees, and Natalie Imbruglia—all hail from Oz.

The names of their tunes alone explain Midnight Oil's status as one-hitters: "Profiteers," "Armistice Day," "Put Down That Weapon," and "White Skin Black Heart." All right, during the Vietnam Era, *maybe,* but during the 80s and 90s, no way. If there's one thing pop/rock music has demonstrated over the past 30 years it's that the Top 40's appetite for, and interest in, songs about social justice and outrage on the streets hovers somewhere around zero. Bob Dylan's "Subterranean Homesick Blues," The Buffalo Springfield's "For What It's Worth," and Peter, Paul & Mary's "If I Had a Hammer"—these singles that resonated in the 60s would have fallen largely on deaf ears in the 80s and 90s.

In the winter of 2002, having been dropped by Columbia Records, Peter Garrett & Co. released *Capricornia* on Liquid 8, a small label based in Minnetonka, Minnesota. It was their twelfth CD of original material, and the lads from Down Under toured extensively throughout Europe, the United States, and of course, Australia, in support of their latest effort.

#86

"What I Am" by Edie Brickell & New Bohemians, 1989

I'm not aware of too many things
I know what I know if you know what I mean

Peaked nationally at #7
Lead singer: Edie Brickell
Written by Kenny Withrow and Edie Brickell

But even if you are just a one-hit wonder, it doesn't stop you from making music. You're still gonna make songs, whether they're going to be hits or not.
　　　—EDIE BRICKELL, AS QUOTED IN *THE AUSTIN CHRONICLE,*
　　　JUNE 2, 2000

The year 1989 provided little in the way of enduring one-hit wonders—songs such as "I Beg Your Pardon" by Kon Kan, Jive Bunny & the Mixmasters' "Swing the Mood," and "Don't Close Your Eyes" by Kix are best forgotten. There was, however, a measure of radio relief in the form of a jangly single featuring Jerry Garcia–like guitar riffs. The tune was called "What I Am," and it was a Top 10 smash for Edie Brickell & New Bohemians.

Oddly enough for a band out of Texas, their breakout hit, which appeared on their debut album, *Shooting Rubberbands at the Stars,* was recorded at Rockfield Studios in Monmouth, Wales, of all places. The outfit was evidently striving for that distinctive late 80s Tex-Welsh sound. A year after issuing 1989's *Shooting Rubberbands at the Stars,* Edie Brickell & New Bohemians released *Ghost of a Dog.* This second album, which failed to generate any buzz, proved to be the group's last.

In the fall of 1988, Edie Brickell & New Bohemians sang "What I Am" on *Saturday Night Live.* Six years later, in October of 1994, Brickell performed by herself on *SNL,* doing a song called "Green," a track from her first solo LP, *Picture Perfect Morning.* "Green" never caught a sniff of the Top 40.

> If you dig deeply into one-hit wonderdom, the nuggets you unearth are both fascinating and surprising. For example, millions of listeners know that Emerson, Lake & Palmer waxed some classic albums back in the 70s, including *Brain Salad Surgery, Pictures at an Exhibition,* as well as their eponymous debut, *Emerson, Lake & Palmer.* However, for all the marvelous music ELP created, the trio made just a solitary visit to the Top 40, that being in the fall of 1972 with "From the Beginning," a song that only spent two weeks on the charts, peaking at #39. "Lucky Man," "Benny the Bouncer," "I Believe in Father Christmas," and "Karn Evil 9" (better known as "Welcome Back My Friends to the Show That Never Ends"), although memorable FM staples, never penetrated the Top 40.

By the way, in 1992, Edie Brickell married Paul Simon. The native of Oak Cliff, Texas—which also happens to be the hometown of guitarist Jimmie Vaughan, the brother of Stevie Ray Vaughan—is Rhymin' Simon's junior by 25 years, although she may very well have a few inches on her husband. Brickell and Simon are the parents of two children, a boy and a girl.

Given the support of such a heavyweight musical spouse, it's surprising that Brickell never again managed to dent the charts after such a promising start with "What I Am." Of all the terrific one-hitters on our tour, Edie Brickell & New Bohemians is perhaps the act that most begs the question, What happened? A tune like "Circle," for example, had "smash" written all over it, the perfect follow-up single to "What I Am." You still have to wonder if the suits over at Geffen Records ever fully realized just what a fresh, marketable sound they had back in the late 80s and early 90s with this band from the Lone Star State.

Finally, fans of Tom Cruise undoubtedly remember his 1989 movie, *Born on the Fourth of July*. What few will recall, though, is that Edie Brickell appeared briefly in that film as a folk singer in a Syracuse bar.

#85

"Magic" by Pilot, 1975

Lazy day in bed, music in my head
Crazy music playing in the morning light

Peaked nationally at #5
Lead singer: David Paton
Written by Billy Lyall and David Paton

The essential difference, however, between Pilot and the twee, tartan-trousered twits that were the [Bay City] Rollers was that Pilot actually had some talent.

—FIRSTFOOT.COM

Pilot was a band from Edinburgh, the Scottish city of 500,000 on the Firth of Forth. The line-up at the time of their #5 smash, "Magic," was Ian Bairnson, Nick Heath, Billy Lyall, David Paton, and Stuart Tosh.

Remember "Smooth," Santana's #1 monster from 1999? This tune, which featured Matchbox Twenty's Rob Thomas on vocals, spent an unbelievable 50 weeks in the Top 40, and it was lauded up and down by both music critics and listeners for Carlos Santana's usual brilliant axe work. Listen to the opening guitar riff—pure rock 'n' roll. The last thing anyone would have called "bubblegum," right? Absolutely, but Carlos's starting lick also happened to be practically a pure lift from Pilot's "Magic," a track long derided for being goofy AM fluff.

If ever a song deserved to have pop/rock fans come to its defense, it would have to be "Magic." The single, quite frankly, has never been given its rightful props. Here was a number that was produced by Alan Parsons, the same man who engineered The Beatles' legendary *Abbey Road,* as well as Pink Floyd's *Dark Side of the Moon.* Not a bad pedigree to bring to a bubblegum record. Yet, despite an all-star producer, David Paton's solid lead singing, an infectious, extremely memorable "wo ho ho it's magic" refrain, and crisp, high-energy guitar playing, Pilot's tune ended up on a 1993 compilation CD entitled *Guilty Pleasures,* the implication being that

What did Pilot and Big Country have in common? Both were Scottish one-hit wonders. The former, as we know, hailed from Edinburgh, the latter, remembered for their 1983 record "In a Big Country," from Dunfermline. By the way, one-hitter Danny Wilson ("Mary's Prayer") was from Dundee, Scotland.

Other Top 40 groups from the land of kilts, trainspotters, and single malt whisky have included Simple Minds ("Don't You Forget About Me" and "Alive & Kicking"); Stealers Wheel ("Stuck in the Middle with You"); and Average White Band ("Pick Up the Pieces" and "Cut the Cake").

"Magic" was somehow a song one would be embarrassed to actually admit to enjoying.

From 1974 through 1977, Pilot issued five albums: *Pilot (From the Album of the Same Name)*, *Second Flight, January, Morin Heights,* and *Two's a Crowd.* "Magic" appeared on their first release. Incidentally, the Scots followed up their Top 5 hit with a single called "January," which was a disappointment, running out of steam at #87. Interestingly, though, "January" went all the way to #1 on the U.K. charts.

After Pilot disbanded in the late 70s, their members remained active in the music business. Drummer Stuart Tosh joined 10cc, the English outfit best recalled for "I'm Not in Love" and "The Things We Do for Love." Billy Lyall struck out on his own, waxing an LP called *Solo Casting* before joining the British popsters known as Dollar. Sadly, Lyall died of AIDS in 1989. As for David Paton, he went on to work primarily as a bassist with the likes of Elton John, Kate Bush, and The Pretenders.

#84

"Tender Love" by Force M.D.'s, 1986

Tender love, love so tender
Pulling me close to you, baby, I surrender

Peaked nationally at #10
Lead singer: Group harmony
Written by Jimmy Jam and Terry Lewis

Sheila E. and Blair Underwood starred in *Krush Groove,* a 1985 film that told the story of the early days of the East Coast rap music scene. While the flick never really found an audience, its soundtrack spawned "Tender Love," a Top 10 single that ranks among the prettiest songs of the 80s.

Certain tunes succeed because they're understated and don't try to do too much—"Tender Love" is such a tune. The classic one-hitter "Back for Good" by Take That is another. Force M.D.'s, like Take That, knew they had a lovely, ear-catching melody to work with, so they wisely dialed back the vocals. The result was extremely pleasing, a record with a restrained feel that wore well play after play, and that didn't feel the need to whack the listener over the head.

Force M.D.'s hailed from New York City, the borough of Staten Island to be precise, and at the time of "Tender Love," they were composed of Jesse Daniels, Antoine Lundy, Stevie Lundy, Charles Nelson, and Trisco Pearson. Although the outfit came together in 1983, their sound possessed a distinct early 70s vibe—you could definitely hear the influence of The Chi-Lites ("Oh Girl" and "Have You Seen Her?") and The Stylistics ("I'm Stone in Love with You" and "Betcha by Golly, Wow"), not to mention Smokey Robinson & The Miracles ("The Tears of a Clown"). For a band with such a smooth R&B style, it was somewhat ironic that their lone Top 40 hit became associated with the *Krush Groove* soundtrack, an album heavily laden with rappers such as Run-DMC, LL Cool J, and The Beastie Boys. In fact, Force M.D.'s were often described as a rap group, which was inaccurate. Granted, on *Love Letters,* their first CD, there

---

As a center for pop music going all the way back to Tin Pan Alley in the 1910s and 1920s, it comes as no surprise that New York City has produced a slew of one-hitters over the years. In addition to Force M.D.'s, here are some memorable one-hit wonders who called The Big Apple home: Gregory Abbott ("Shake You Down"), Brooklyn Bridge ("Worst That Could Happen"), Deee-Lite ("Groove Is in the Heart"), Ace Frehley ("New York Groove"), Jellybean ("Sidewalk Talk"), New York City ("I'm Doin' Fine Now"), Stories ("Brother Louie"), 2 in a Room ("Wiggle It"), and Suzanne Vega ("Luka").

was a modicum of hip-hop flava, but over the years, the group's primary stock-in-trade had always been soulful, urban rhythm and blues.

In 2000, a Force M.D.'s LP called *The Reunion* was issued on the Mad Love label. Absent, though, were Jesse Daniels, Stevie Lundy, Antoine Lundy, and Charles Nelson, the latter two, sadly, having died in 1998 and 1995, respectively. The only holdover from the "Tender Love" days was Trisco Pearson. Not much of a "reunion," really.

Today, "Tender Love" is available on a variety of compilations, including *Slow Jams, The 80's: Funky Love,* and *Smooth Grooves: New Jack Ballads, Vol. 2.* And, for those who are into cover versions of one-hit wonders, check out a compact disc entitled *Shake What Ya Mama Gave Ya: Hot New Rump-Shakin Hits,* the eleventh cut on which is "Tender Love" done by an obscure outfit called Legal Tender.

#83

"Barely Breathing" by Duncan Sheik, 1997

'Cause I am barely breathing
And I can't find the air

Peaked nationally at #16
Lead singer: Duncan Sheik
Written by Duncan Sheik

The Florida Marlins won the World Series in 1997, edging the Cleveland Indians four games to three. And if you thought a Fall Classic pitting the Marlins against the Tribe was wacky and improbable, how about the one-hit wonders from '97? "Tubthumping" by Chumbawamba—an eccentric song about "pissing the night away." OMC's "How Bizarre"—a mysterious number concerning, among other things, 1969 Chevrolets, Marines, and clowns. Of course, there was also "Barbie Girl" by a group from Denmark dubbed Aqua. On the less zany side of the one-hit fence, 1997 spawned Fiona Apple and "Criminal," "Lovefool" by The Cardigans, The Verve Pipe's "The Freshmen," as well as the next stop on our musical tour, a track entitled "Barely Breathing" by Duncan Sheik.

"Barely Breathing" quietly entered the Top 40 in early February of '97, and it remained a chart fixture for the next 10 months, peaking at #16. With its acoustic guitar and clear, earnest vocals, the record wore incredibly well. Like "Breakfast at Tiffany's" by Deep Blue Something and Shawn Mullins's "Lullaby," this was the sort of mid- to late-90s one-hitter that FM radio put into super heavy rotation, yet surprisingly, listeners never seemed to tire of it. Some songs run a sprint, quickly flaming out; others, such as "Barely Breathing," are marathoners that stay the course, then gradually and gracefully fade away. By the way, when Duncan Sheik's smash single finally exited the Top 40 after an astounding 42 weeks, it spent another 13 weeks in the Top 100. When the turntable finally stopped spinning, "Barely Breathing" had, according to *Billboard* magazine, enjoyed the fourth-longest chart run in pop history. Not bad for a one hit wonder.

A native of New Jersey, Sheik resided for much of his childhood in the resort town of Hilton Head, South Carolina, before heading off to attend Brown University in Providence, Rhode Island. Interestingly, while as a student at Brown, he played lead guitar in a band called Liz & Lisa. The Liz of the group was Liz Mitchell, while Lisa was her roommate, Lisa Loeb, who, of course, scored a #1 hit for herself in 1994 with "Stay (I Missed You)." After graduating from college, Sheik devoted several years to honing his skills as a songwriter, the culmination of which was his 1996 debut album, *Duncan Sheik*, the third cut on which was "Barely Breathing." His sophomore effort, *Humming*, was issued in '98, followed by *Phantom Moon* and *Daylight*, released in 2001 and 2002, respectively. Four full-length CDs under his belt, and Duncan Sheik is still working toward that elusive second hit single.

Brent's Two Cents: Having never personally seen the guy's Garden State birth certificate, I can't say with 100 percent certainty that his real name is, in fact, Duncan Sheik, but he claims it is, and that's good enough for me.

What about one-hitter David Essex, who scored a #5 record in 1974 with "Rock On"? He was actually born David Cook. Maria Muldaur of "Midnight at the Oasis" fame? Maria D'Amato. As for Rick Derringer, whose lone hit was "Rock & Roll, Hoochie Koo," well, his real name was Richard Zehringer. And, finally, Marc Bolan, the leader of one-hitters T. Rex ("Bang a Gong [Get It On]")? How does Mark Feld grab you!

#82

"Turning Japanese" by The Vapors, 1980

Everyone around me is a total stranger
Everyone avoids me like a psyched Lone Ranger—
        everyone!

Peaked nationally at #36
Lead singer: Dave Fenton
Written by Dave Fenton

When this song hit the airwaves, a rumor spread in the U.S. that it was about masturbation, and that "turning Japanese" was a reference to the facial expression made at the moment of climax.

            —RADIOMOI.COM REVIEW OF "TURNING JAPANESE"

The Vapors chose the perfect name for their band, as it effectively captured the ethereal, here-today-gone-tomorrow quality of this early

80s New Wave one-hit wonder. Although "Turning Japanese" barely scratched the surface of the American Top 40 charts, it raced all the way to #3 in The Vapors' native England.

Along with the Divinyls' "I Touch Myself," this record is among the all-time great singles exploring the subject of, well, how can we put this delicately—pleasuring one's self. "Turning Japanese" originally appeared on The Vapors' debut album, *New Clear Days,* which featured an astonishing 19 tracks. The outfit actually only issued two LPs of original material during their brief (1978 through 1981) existence: the aforementioned *New Clear Days* followed by *Magnets.* However, it's worth noting that in the past decade, no fewer than three "best of" collections have been released: *Anthology* (1995), *Turning Japanese: The Best of The Vapors* (1996), and *Vaporized* (1998). Naturally, "Turning Japanese" is highlighted on all these compilation CDs. The song also pops up on numerous movie soundtracks, including *Romy & Michele's High School Reunion, Major League 3: Back to the Minors, Beverly Hills Ninja,* as well as *Charlie's Angels.*

The Vapors were composed of Edward Bazalgette (guitar), Dave Fenton (vocals), Howard Smith (drums), and Steve Smith (bass). Interestingly, most listeners thought Dave Fenton was singing about "a cyclone ranger." Huh? Actually, his exact words were "a psyched Lone Ranger." Ah, okay, Dave, *that* explains it. By the way, prior to forming The Vapors, Fenton worked as a solicitor, what the Brits call a lawyer. And, actually, according to all current reports out of the U.K., Fenton is back toiling in the legal field today, with an emphasis on music law.

Indie rocker Liz Phair included a cover of "Turning Japanese" on her 1995 album, *Juvenilia.* Of course, The Vindictives' version, issued in '96, is considered an underground classic, primarily because it appears on a CD called *Party Time for Assholes.*

You might be surprised to learn how many tunes actually feature the word "Japanese" in their titles. Ween, the eccentric duo from Pennsylvania, released a country number in 1996 entitled "Japanese Cowboy." Jazz legend Duke Ellington recorded a song back in the 20s called "Japanese Dream." The Texas space rockers, Mazinga Phaser, gave us "Japanese Space Opera." None of these records, though, is about masturbation—at least not as far as we can determine.

Brent's Two Cents: Because of the salacious and mysterious nature of The Vapors' Top 40 hit, it's been the subject of endless Internet chatter. Check out this frantic query from expost.com: "About 'Turning Japanese' by The Vapors—is it really about masturbation? And if so, how?? I don't understand how those lyrics could have anything to do with masturbation!!"

Of course, there can only be one reply to this post: "Wanker!"

#81

"Counting Blue Cars" by Dishwalla, 1996

Tell me all your thoughts on God
'Cause I am on my way to meet Her

Peaked nationally at #15
Lead singer: JR Richards
Written by Scot Alexander, Rodney Browning,
      Greg Kolanek, George Pendergast, and JR Richards

Some of the best stuff we play is completely an accident.
We've got no idea what we're doing. That's why we're
trying to unlearn everything we've ever learned, so we
can make more mistakes and get better.
      —RODNEY BROWNING, DISHWALLA'S LEAD GUITARIST

Dishwalla? Sounds like the name of a dusty town in the Australian Outback, but it's actually the curious moniker of a band from Santa

Barbara, California. What's that you say? You've never heard of them? Well, perhaps you recall their lone hit, "Counting Blue Cars," a single that spent more than eight months in the Top 40, a track that in 1996 earned *Billboard* magazine's "Rock Song of the Year" honors. "Counting Blue Cars," huh?

Yes, the group is called Dishwalla and they rose from obscurity in the summer of '96 on the strength of "Counting Blue Cars," a #15 record that millions of FM listeners from Portland, Maine, to Portland, Oregon, referred to as the "tell me all your thoughts on God" song. Like another memorable 90s one-hit single, "One of Us" by Joan Osborne, "Counting Blue Cars" invited people to take a fresh look at the way in which they approached religion and spirituality.

"Counting Blue Cars" came off *Pet Your Friends,* Dishwalla's eccentrically named second album. The tune has also appeared on several CD collections, including *Unusual Suspects, 93.7 Edge: The Best of 1996,* and *Unstoppable 90s: Alternative.* The boys from Southern California have landed on numerous motion picture soundtracks as well. Their "Find Your Way Back" was featured in *American Pie,* "Truth Serum" in *The Avengers,* and "The Thrill Is Gone" in the Andy Garcia

---

Santa Barbara, Dishwalla's hometown, is approximately 100 miles north of Los Angeles and 340 miles south of San Francisco. Over the years, the Golden State has produced many memorable one-hitters, acts such as Karla Bonoff ("Personally"), The Chantays ("Pipeline"), Alan O'Day ("Undercover Angel"), Joey Scarbury ("Theme from 'Greatest American Hero' [Believe It or Not]"), Vicki Lawrence ("The Night the Lights Went Out in Georgia"), Timex Social Club ("Rumors"), Charlene ("I've Never Been to Me"), Lee Ritenour ("Is It You"), Randy Newman ("Short People"), Les Crane ("Desiderata"), Pacific Gas & Electric ("Are You Ready?"), The Surfaris ("Wipe Out"), and The Cascades ("Rhythm of the Rain").

flick *Things to Do in Denver When You're Dead*. In addition, in 1994, a year before *Pet Your Friends* was issued, Dishwalla covered Karen and Richard Carpenter's "It's Going to Take Some Time" on a tribute compact disc called *If I Were a Carpenter*.

To date, the band has four albums to their credit: *Dishwalla* (1995), *Pet Your Friends* (1995), *And You Think You Know What Life's About* (1998), and *Opaline* (2002). And even though Dishwalla never became a Top 40 juggernaut, they continue to be a popular live act, gigging at venues like The Canyon Theater in Agoura Hills, California; the Stone Pony in Asbury Park, New Jersey; and The Village Underground in New York City.

#80

"Everyone's Gone to the Moon" by Jonathan King, 1965

Streets full of people, all alone
Roads full of houses, never home

Peaked nationally at #17
Lead singer: Jonathan King
Written by Jonathan King

He's a sabra. A "sabra" is an Israeli fruit that's prickly on the outside and all soft and lovely inside. That's Jonathan King.

—BRITISH TELEVISION HOST JIMMY SAVILE DESCRIBING
HIS FRIEND, JONATHAN KING

London native Jonathan King was only 21 years old when he basked for the first, and only, time in the Top 40 spotlight. The song that propelled him to fame was called "Everyone's Gone to the Moon," a dreamy, melancholy number that peaked at #17, spending seven weeks on the charts.

No two ways about it, this was a sad record, a lament about human isolation, loneliness, and depersonalization in the face of a rapidly changing world. At the same time, though, "Everyone's Gone to the Moon" possessed an undeniable beauty, what with its lush violins and King's light, innocent-sounding lead vocals. By the way, Chad & Jeremy, the British duo best recalled for 1964's "A Summer Song," waxed a relatively well-received version of this track. Their take, however, veered off in a more upbeat direction, in the process draining the tune of its intrinsic mournfulness, the exact element that made the original so atmospheric and effective. The best "Everyone's Gone to the Moon" cover was actually laid down in the year 2000 by an eccentric outfit out of Oklahoma City called The Flaming Lips. Although mostly piano-based, this version beautifully captured the sweet sadness of King's Top 20 hit.

Surprisingly, a Jonathan King album was never issued in the mid-60s to capitalize on his single's success. In fact, it wasn't until 2001 with the release of a CD entitled *Hedgehoppers Anonymous* that "Everyone's Gone to the Moon" appeared on an LP under King's name. Indeed, in a musical career spanning some 40 years, the Englishman's only two albums are the aforementioned *Hedgehoppers Anonymous* and 1973's *Pandora's Box*. "Everyone's Gone to the Moon" has naturally made its way onto numerous compact disc collections, including *Back to the Sixties, The Woodstock Generation: Everything Is Beautiful,* and *The British Invasion: History of British Rock, Vol. 7.*

After hitting chart paydirt in '65, King spent the remainder of the decade behind the scenes, mostly scouting for new talent on behalf of the Decca label. His greatest discovery was a group composed of Tony Banks, Phil Collins, Peter Gabriel, Anthony Phillips, Mike Rutherford, and Chris Stewart—the outfit dubbed Genesis. King is also credited with spawning 10cc. The Bay City Rollers, the popsters from Edinburgh, Scotland, remembered for "Saturday Night," a #1 smash from late 1975, were another Jonathan King find.

Unfortunately, this one-hit wonder's story does not have a happy ending. Here's what *The Guardian* newspaper reported on November 22, 2001: "Jonathan King, the millionaire pop impresario, was beginning a seven-year prison sentence last night for sexually abusing teenage boys throughout the 1980s. King, 56, was visibly shaken as he received his sentence at the Old Bailey for four indecent assaults and two more serious sexual offences on schoolboys aged 14 and 15."

#79

"Voices Carry" by 'til tuesday, 1985

Hush, hush, keep it down now
Voices carry

Peaked nationally at #8
Lead singer: Aimee Mann
Written by Michael Hausman, Robert Holmes,
    Aimee Mann, and Joey Pesce

With her blonde hair and icy, brittle words, Aimee Mann
is like Janeane Garofalo disguised as Uma Thurman.
—CNN.COM/ENTERTAINMENT, AUGUST 28, 2002

Like k.d. lang, 'til tuesday, for reasons that were never fully articulated, were rockers who preferred lowercase letters over upper. The group, a New Wave outfit from Boston, was composed of Michael Hausman, Robert Holmes, Aimee Mann, and Joey Pesce. During its run from 1983 through 1989, 'til tuesday issued three albums: *Voices Carry* (1985), *Welcome Home* (1986), and *Everything's Different Now* (1988). Their Top 10 hit, "Voices Carry," was, of course, culled from their '85 release.

It's interesting to note the names of two of the many compilation

CDs that featured "Voices Carry": *18 New Wave Classics* and *Just Can't Get Enough: New Wave Hits of the '80s.* So, what exactly is, or more accurately *was,* this style of music dubbed New Wave, and how did 'til tuesday fit into the picture?

Well, first of all, the New Wave era spanned, in very broad terms, from 1979 to 1986, so "Voices Carry" arrived as the curtain was coming down on the genre. In terms of one-hit wonders, look at the period as beginning with M's "Pop Muzik" and Gary Numan's "Cars" and ending with Baltimora's "Tarzan Boy" and Scritti Politti's "Perfect Way," with the years '82, '83, and '84 being New Wave's real salad days.

New Wave was essentially a spirited response to the Soft Rock and Disco that dominated the mid- to late 70s. To be sure, acts such as The Eagles, Hall & Oates, Ambrosia, Jackson Browne, Donna Summer, and the Bee Gees waxed some terrific, memorable sides during Jimmy Carter's presidency, yet listeners were yearning for a new sound—something quirkier, edgier, more experimental. Enter the likes of Adam Ant, The Cars, Culture Club, The Knack, Simple Minds, Thompson Twins, and of course, 'til tuesday. To understand the dif-

---

New Wave spawned some of pop music's classic one-hit wonders, artists who are vividly remembered today: Dexys Midnight Runners ("Come on Eileen"), Nena ("99 Luftballons"), and Thomas Dolby ("She Blinded Me with Science"), to name just a few. What follows, though, is a sampling of relatively obscure New Wave one-hitters, acts you may have forgotten about: Bram Tchaikovsky ("Girl of My Dreams"), Haircut One Hundred ("Love Plus One"), Icicle Works ("Whisper to a Scream [Birds Fly]"), JoBoxers ("Just Got Lucky"), Re-Flex ("The Politics of Dancing"), Romeo Void ("A Girl in Trouble [Is a Terrible Thing]"), The Style Council ("My Ever Changing Mood"), and Tom Tom Club ("Genius of Love").

ference between old school 70s pop and 80s New Wave, all you have to do is lend an ear to, say, The Commodores' "Three Times a Lady," a #1 smash from 1978, and then listen immediately to "(Keep Feeling) Fascination" by the Human League, a Top 10 record from 1983.

Leaning heavily on synthesizers and a pounding, robotic beat, "Voices Carry" was the quintessential New Wave song. In addition, Aimee Mann's cool, dark lead vocals were right in step with the style. The tune's accompanying video was pure New Wave, as well, replete with spiky hairdos, black clothing, and gauzy, atmospheric lighting—perfect for MTV and VH-1 consumption.

By the way, 'til tuesday might never have risen to prominence if they hadn't won WBCN-FM's "1983 Rock and Roll Rumble." Every year, WBCN, a popular Boston radio station, hosts a battle of the bands, and back in '83, 'til tuesday beat out the likes of the Del Fuegos, Jerry's Kids, and Lizzie Borden & the Axes to take home first prize.

#78

"Back for Good" by Take That, 1995

Whatever I said, whatever I did, I didn't mean it
I just want you back for good

Peaked nationally at #7
Lead singer: Gary Barlow
Written by Gary Barlow

Gary Barlow, Howard Donald, Jason Orange, Mark Owen, and Robbie Williams—these five young Englishmen were known as Take That, and from 1990 to 1996 they were the undisputed Kings of Pop in their native U.K., selling tens of millions of records and reeling off a string of #1 British singles. Here in the States, however, the group is remembered as quintessential 1990s one-hit wonders, a boy band that landed at #7 with a song called "Back for Good."

Take That's lone U.S. hit spent a solid 25 weeks in the Top 40. Featuring Gary Barlow's soulful, assured lead vocals, which were a blend of George Michael and Elton John, coupled with outstanding background harmonies, "Back for Good" was easily among the best tunes of the 90s.

Like "Into the Night" by Benny Mardones, another classic one-hitter, this track possesses a timeless, evergreen quality—"Back for Good" will sound as fresh in 2005 as it did in 1995. Interestingly, a lot of music from the mid-90s has held up well into the new millennium. Songs like "Ironic" and "Hand in My Pocket" by Alanis Morissette; "Wonderwall" and "Champagne Supernova" by Oasis; and Natalie Merchant's "Carnival" and "Wonder"—all of these hit singles from '95 and '96 have aged gracefully.

As mentioned earlier, Take That was a so-called "boy band," a label that has often been used derisively. The knock against boy bands—outfits such as *NSYNC, O-Town, Backstreet Boys, and New Kids on the Block—has always been the same: These are manufactured groups of dubious talent, a bunch of good-looking non-musicians who appeal only to 12-year-old girls. But then you hear catchy, well-crafted numbers like the Backstreet Boys' "Quit Playing Games (With My Heart)" or Take That's "Back for Good," and, well, you're kind of forced to admit that, all right, maybe *some* of this boy band stuff is pretty decent.

Boy band bashing is similar to the arguments of legions of people across America who claim to "hate all Rap, especially that no-talent

---

Take That. How about Take 6, an outfit from Alabama known for their jazzy gospel sound. Then there was Take It, an obscure punk band from the 70s. And let's not forget these groups: Take One, Take Two, Take Five, Take Dake, and Shi-Take.

Eminem." Then, in October of 2000, millions unexpectedly found themselves digging Eminem as he hip-hopped his way through "Stan" on *Saturday Night Live,* and suddenly opinions softened from Spokane to Savannah: "Hey, did you happen to catch Eminem on *SNL*? He was surprisingly good, don't you think? I'm gonna pick up one of his CDs later this week."

After Take That called it a day in 1996, Gary Barlow decided to pursue a solo career. To date, he's waxed two albums, 1997's *Open Road* and *Twelve Months Eleven Days* from 2001, neither of which spawned any hits on this side of the Atlantic. As for Robbie Williams, the other high-profile member of Take That, he's also released a few solo compact discs: *Life Thru a Lens* (1997), *I've Been Expecting You* (1998), and *Sing When You're Winning* (2000)—nary a chart single, though.

#77

"Shattered Dreams" by Johnny Hates Jazz, 1988

And now you've given me, given me,
Nothing but shattered dreams, shattered dreams

Peaked nationally at #2
Lead singer: Clark Datchler
Written by Clark Datchler

Johnny Hates Jazz was the London trio of Clark Datchler, Calvin Hayes, and Mike Nocito. During their 1986 through 1991 run, they issued two albums of original material, *Turn Back the Clock* (1987) and *Tall Stories* (1991), with their only hit single, "Shattered Dreams," coming off the former. The latter LP, incidentally, featured a guy by the name of Phil Thornalley on lead vocals, as Clark Datchler had by that time left the group to take his chances as a solo artist.

"Shattered Dreams" was a stylish slice of late 80s pop, in the same vein as one-hitters like "Mary's Prayer" by Danny Wilson and "Breakout" by Swing Out Sister. It's interesting to note that whenever jazzy, sophisticated records crack the Top 40, they are almost always the products of artists from the U.K. (*e.g.*, Sade, Level 42, Johnny Hates Jazz, Everything But the Girl, Danny Wilson, Simply Red, and Swing Out Sister). Even Basia, the poppy jazzster from Poland remembered best for her 1988 tune "Time and Tide," has strong ties to Britain. Yet America, the birthplace of jazz, the country that spawned Sarah Vaughan and Ella Fitzgerald, has had virtually no luck—or perhaps it's a matter of having close to zero *interest*—in turning out its own Sades, Basias, and Danny Wilsons. *Johnny* Hates Jazz? It's more like *Omaha* Hates Jazz.

The thing that makes "Shattered Dreams" such a memorable song is its insistent, understated groove. This is a track that moves quickly, but subtly. Plus, Clark Datchler coolly swings the vocal in that elegant manner that seems to be the sole province of British pop singers. Memo to the Whitney Houstons, Mariah Careys, Celine Dions, and Michael Boltons of the musical world: Quit yelling! Does *every* number have to be belted? The word is "finesse."

"Shattered Dreams," which peaked at #2 and spent 13 weeks on the charts, has appeared on more than a dozen CD compilations, in-

---

Alison Moyet ("Invisible"), Status Quo ("Pictures of Matchstick Men"), Spandau Ballet ("True"), Tracey Ullman ("They Don't Know"), and Big Country ("In a Big Country") are all one-hit wonders. What else do these artists have in common? Well, on July 13th of 1985, a Saturday, they each took part in Live Aid at London's Wembley Stadium. And, just in case you were wondering, Tracey Ullman did *not* sing that day, rather, she spoke at the event.

cluding *Rock On: 1988, Pop & Wave, Vol. 6,* and *Living in Oblivion: The 80's Greatest Hits, Vol. 3.* The *Pop & Wave, Vol. 6* album, by the way, deserves special one-hit wonder commendation because, in addition to Johnny Hates Jazz, it highlights no fewer than four classic one-hitters: a-ha ("Take on Me"), Baltimora ("Tarzan Boy"), Double ("The Captain of Her Heart"), and Love and Rockets ("So Alive").

It bears mentioning that Clark Datchler and Calvin Hayes, who played drums and keyboards, respectively, for Johnny Hates Jazz, both came from highly musical families. Clark's father, Fred Datchler, was a member of the Polka Dots and The Stargazers, popular English jazz outfits in the 40s and 50s. As for Calvin Hayes, his dad is Mickie Most, the well-respected rock 'n' roll producer from the 1960s, a fellow who worked with acts ranging from Lulu ("To Sir with Love") to The Animals ("Don't Let Me Be Misunderstood") to Donovan ("Wear Your Love Like Heaven").

#76

"Seasons in the Sun" by Terry Jacks, 1974

Good-bye to you my trusted friend
We've known each other since we were nine or ten

Peaked nationally at #1
Lead singer: Terry Jacks
Written by Jacques Brel and Rod McKuen

Maudlin and mawkish. Sappy and sentimental. Cheesy and schmaltzy. Yes, Terry Jacks's song was all of those things. But, at the same time, it was also just a damn good record.

Was there ever a Top 40 track with a more memorable opening? There was that foreboding, descending bass riff: "boom . . . boom . . . boom . . . boom . . ."—the beginning notes that helped "Seasons in the Sun" sell more than 11 million copies worldwide.

The fascinating story of this #1 smash begins in the early 60s with Jacques Brel, the colorful Brussels-born singer and songwriter. Brel had penned a tune in French called "Le Moribond," a dying man's heartbreaking *adieu* to his father, his wife, Francoise, as well as his best friend, Emile, who, incidentally, had been sleeping with Francoise. Enter Rod McKuen, the poet, singer, and songwriter from California. McKuen took "Le Moribond" and translated it into English, calling his new creation "Seasons in the Sun."

Rod McKuen passed his tune on to The Kingston Trio, the San Francisco folkies who reached #1 with their "Tom Dooley" back in 1958. The Kingston Trio waxed a version of "Seasons in the Sun," featuring a clear, energetic acoustic guitar that lent it a real Spanish flavor. Chartwise, the tune stiffed.

Fast forward to the early 70s. The Beach Boys—yes, Brian Wilson & Co.—are in a recording studio laying down their own take on "Seasons in the Sun." This cover is never issued. However, also in the studio that day is Terry Jacks, a young Canadian who had actually brought "Seasons in the Sun" to the attention of the Southern Californians.

A bright Top 40 light bulb—*ping!*—must have gone off in Jacks's head during his time spent with The Beach Boys, because he decided to record the Jacques Brel–Rod McKuen composition himself, and the result, of course, was a one-hitter for the ages.

By the way, if you place the Terry Jacks "Seasons in the Sun" next to The Kingston Trio's, you'll immediately notice several differences. For example, while Papa is present in both versions, Jacks jettisons Francoise, the cheating spouse. The 1961 and 1974 cuts both mention the "trusted friend," although only The Kingston Trio calls him by name, Emile. Also, Terry Jacks ratchets up the Kleenex factor by introducing a young girl, Michelle, into the equation. Overall, Jacks's rendition is less earthy and infinitely more bubblegum than the Trio's.

Incidentally, in 1970—four years before "Seasons in the Sun" dominated the AM dial and made Terry Jacks famous, or, at least, *semi-famous* and rich—Jacks twice tasted chart success as a member of The Poppy Family: first, when that outfit landed at #2 with "Which Way You Goin' Billy?" in the spring of '70, and then later that same year when they peaked at #29 with "That's Where I Went Wrong." Terry Jacks's then wife, Susan, sang lead vocals on both numbers—in fact, the labels on the 45s read *The Poppy Family (Featuring Susan Jacks)*.

Brent's Two Cents: Is Terry Jacks and his "Seasons in the Sun" the best one-hitter from the 1970s? I think most Top 40 fans, myself included, would answer that question with a "no." Personally, I'd rate 70s one-hit wonders like "Lotta Love" by Nicolette Larson, Ace's "How Long," and "Dancing in the Moonlight" by King Harvest ahead of "Seasons in the Sun." That being said, a strong case could be made for calling Terry Jacks's #1 monster the most *memorable* one-hitter from the 70s, as *everyone* vividly recalls this 30-year-old AM classic.

#75

"Key Largo" by Bertie Higgins, 1982

We had it all
Just like Bogie and Bacall

Peaked nationally at #8
Lead singer: Bertie Higgins
Written by Bertie Higgins and Sonny Limbo

Remember those story songs from the 60s and 70s? "Billy, Don't Be a Hero" by Bo Donaldson and the Heywoods. Paper Lace's "The Night Chicago Died." "Ode to Billie Joe" by Bobbie Gentry. Vicki Lawrence's

"The Night the Lights Went Out in Georgia." Sure, those tunes could be silly and corny, but they were also a lot of fun and highly memorable. In 1982, another record with a story to tell—a single that would have felt very much at home in, say, 1974—climbed the charts: "Key Largo" by Elbert "Bertie" Higgins, the pride of Tarpon Springs, Florida.

"Key Largo" told of a couple's romantic history against the black and white backdrop of *Key Largo*, the 1948 film starring Humphrey Bogart and Lauren Bacall. It was a simple song, really. The fact that it reached #8 and spent a solid 17 weeks in the Top 40 is a testament to the power of pop culture imagery. "Bogie and Bacall"—the phrase itself is magical and iconic. Higgins also tossed in a "Here's looking at you, kid," just for good measure, even though that famous line was from *Casablanca*, a movie that paired Bogart *not* with Lauren Bacall, but rather with Ingrid Bergman. Speaking of the 1942 silver screen classic, on his album *Just Another Day in Paradise*, in addition to "Key Largo," Higgins also included a track called "Casablanca."

By the time the name Bertie Higgins became known to radio listeners, the Floridian was in his mid-30s. However, he had been toiling as a professional musician since 1963, when he started drumming with an outfit called The Roemans, who were the backing band for Tommy Roe, the singer from Atlanta best recalled for the 1969 bubblegum hits "Dizzy" and "Jam Up Jelly Tight."

Interestingly enough, apart from their work with Tommy Roe, The Roemans, originally known as Lanny and The Impressions, waxed a half-dozen of their own 45s, one of which featured "Miserlou" as the A-side. "Miserlou," of course, is the legendary surf instrumental that has been covered literally dozens of times over the years, most notably by the Southern California guitarist Dick Dale.

When The Roemans called it a day in 1970, Higgins went into musical hibernation for more than a decade before surfacing in '82 with his *Just Another Day in Paradise* LP and striking paydirt with "Key Largo." However, even the creative spirit and energy of Bogie and Bacall couldn't carry over to a follow-up hit single, and by 1983, the public was asking, "Bertie who?"

These days, Higgins resides just north of St. Petersburg, in his hometown of Tarpon Springs, and he's still making music as the leader of Bertie Higgins & The Band of Pirates. The group actively gigs around the world, playing to large, enthusiastic audiences from Las Vegas to Tokyo.

Brent's Two Cents: The early 80s were dotted with one-hit wonders such as Charlie Dore ("Pilot of the Airwaves"), Johnny Lee ("Lookin' for Love"), Terri Gibbs ("Somebody's Knockin'"), Joey Scarbury ("Theme from 'Greatest American Hero' [Believe It or Not]"), and Charlene ("I've Never Been to Me"). These were the sort of artists and songs, like Bertie Higgins and his "Key Largo," that were extremely fortunate to have broken through in the period from 1980 to 1982. I say "fortunate" for the simple reason that by 1983, indeed as early as the fall of '82, Top 40 radio had undergone a sea change in terms of its playlist. Easygoing popsters in the vein of Bertie Higgins and Charlene had been rapidly supplanted by techno New Wavers like Soft Cell ("Tainted Love") and After the Fire ("Der Kommissar"). *Adios* Larry Graham ("One in a Million You"), *hola* Kajagoogoo ("Too Shy").

#74

"You Gotta Be" by Des'ree, 1994

Listen as your day unfolds
Challenge what the future holds

Peaked nationally at #5
Lead singer: Des'ree
Written by Ashley Ingram and Des'ree

Des'ree has often expressed her admiration for Billie Holiday, Sarah Vaughan, and Ella Fitzgerald, and from the very first spin, you could definitely hear the influence of these jazz legends in "You Gotta Be," a song that spent an amazing 30 weeks in the Top 40. The singer has also spoken of her mother's love of the Motown sound, and there's no denying that a certain Stevie Wonder and Supremes vibe permeated her hit record, too. In fact, "You Gotta Be" was one of the few chart singles that ever married jazz to soul.

From late '94 through the summer of '95, "You Gotta Be" was omnipresent—duck into your neighborhood deli for a soda and a bag of chips, there was Des'ree coming through loud and clear from the boombox behind the counter; switch on VH-1, there was the pretty singer's video—morning, noon, and night; tune in to *Saturday Night Live* on February 11, 1995, there was Bob Newhart hosting, with our girl, Des'ree, belting out her smash as that evening's musical guest. Taxi cabs, pizza parlors, bars, dorm rooms, department stores, elevators, you name the location, "You Gotta Be" was in the air.

Des'ree's first album, *Mind Adventures,* was released in 1992 to scant notice in America; however, it did include a track called "Feel So High" that rose to #13 in her native England. The interesting thing about "Feel So High" is that it starts off sounding an awful lot like "You Gotta Be," so much so, in fact, that it almost seems as if the former was written and recorded as a dry run for the latter. In 1994, Des'ree issued a CD called *I Ain't Movin',* the first cut of which was

Des'ree was born in London on November 30, 1968. Her parents, incidentally, were natives of Barbados. When you think about it, over the course of the last 40 or so years, the city that has most shaped the sound of pop/rock music in the United States is probably London, England.

Consider just a sampling of the highly influential and popular acts that have sprung from the British capital: Dire Straits, Petula Clark, Eurythmics, T. Rex, Squeeze, The Clash, Dusty Springfield, Sex Pistols, and of course, The Rolling Stones.

"You Gotta Be," and the third, "Feel So High," was recycled from *Mind Adventures.* This recycling of old tunes very much goes to the issue of Des'ree's status as a one-hit wonder, as thus far in her career she just hasn't displayed enough variety and originality in her material. In terms of being a regular visitor to the charts, what good is an impressive set of pipes, which Des'ree undoubtedly possesses, if you don't complement it with fresh, imaginative songwriting?

It's worth noting that "You Gotta Be" was featured on 1997's *Diana, Princess of Wales: Tribute,* a collection that also included Mariah Carey's "Hero," "I'll Fly Away" by Aretha Franklin, and Bruce Springsteen's "Streets of Philadelphia." Des'ree's hit has also found its way onto compilations like *Best of Dance '94, Soul Hits of the 90's,* and *Pop Music: The Modern Era 1976–1999.*

To date, Des'ree, whose full name is Des'ree Weeks, has four LPs to her credit: *Mind Adventures* (1992), *I Ain't Movin'* (1994), *Supernatural* (1998), and *Endangered Species* (2000). Four albums, but still only one Top 40 single.

#73

"Judy in Disguise (With Glasses)" by John Fred & His Playboy Band, 1967

Judy in disguise, well, that's what you are
Lemonade pies, with a brand new car

Peaked nationally at #1
Lead singer: John Fred
Written by Andrew Bernard and John Fred

The Beatles' "Hello, Goodbye" was standing atop the charts in late January of 1968 until "Judy in Disguise (With Glasses)," a tune with a

title aping The Fab Four's own "Lucy in the Sky (With Diamonds),"
came along and claimed the #1 spot for itself.

"Judy in Disguise (With Glasses)" was simply a raucous, puts-a-
smile-on-your-face record. Unlike, say, The Buffalo Springfield's "For
What It's Worth (Stop, Hey What's That Sound)," here was a song
from '67 devoid of any political or social message, other than *shake
your bones and have a good time.*

The intriguing thing about John Fred & His Playboy Band's smash
is the way it defies easy description. It's been called a novelty number, but that's selling the tune way short, although there undoubtedly
is a novelty aspect to it. Others have called it a piece of boppy blue-
eyed soul, which is accurate, to an extent. Actually, probably the best
way to describe "Judy in Disguise (With Glasses)" would be *psyche-
delic bubblegum,* a phrase that might seem oxymoronic, yet, in this
case, fits perfectly. It's a highly unusual single that manages to be
spacey and trippy, while at the same time goofy, sunny, and bouncy.
Again, that rarest of musical hybrids: psychedelic bubblegum.

The downside to waxing "Judy in Disguise (With Glasses)" was
that it painted John Fred & His Playboy Band into a corner in terms of
releasing successful follow-up records, primarily because their #1
hit was in no way representative of the group's core sound, which
was soulful R&B. Naturally, the millions of AM listeners and 45 r.p.m.
buyers who dug "Judy" and vaulted it to the very top of the charts
wanted and expected more of the same. Of course, that would've
been a fool's errand on the part of John Fred & His Playboy Band for
the simple reason that a song as wonderfully quirky and idiosyncratic
as "Judy in Disguise (With Glasses)" was impossible to replicate. So,
instead, this outfit from Baton Rouge, Louisiana, served up their
usual menu of tasty rhythm and blues, but with respect to denting
the Top 40, their R&B offerings fell flat. "Judy" proved to be their first
and last chart single.

Brent's Two Cents: Before researching John Fred & His Playboy Band
for this book, I knew virtually nothing about the group. All I did know

was that "Judy in Disguise (With Glasses)" was a terrific tune, and that there was a certain something in John Fred's lead vocals that reminded me of Dr. John, the one-hit wonder from New Orleans who reached #9 in 1973 with "Right Place, Wrong Time." Well, it turns out that in the late 50s, when Fred was still in high school, he did some recording with a fellow named Mac Rebennack, a singer, guitarist, and pianist who would later adopt the moniker Dr. John.

By the way, in addition to John Fred & His Playboy Band and Dr. John, other one-hitters from the Pelican State include Ernie K-Doe ("Mother-in-Law"/#1 in 1961), Frankie Ford ("Sea Cruise"/#14 in 1959), and Brent Bourgeois ("Dare to Fall in Love"/#32 in 1990).

#72

"Talk It Over" by Grayson Hugh, 1989

Harsh words are spoken
Promises are broken

Peaked nationally at #19
Lead singer: Grayson Hugh
Written by Sandy Linzer and Irwin Levine

Remember a guy named Rick Astley? He enjoyed a string of Top 10 singles in the late 80s with "Never Gonna Give You Up," "Together Forever," and "It Would Take a Strong, Strong Man," the first two of which went all the way to #1. For all the world, Astley sounded like a soulful black crooner from Detroit. Imagine, then, the surprise when his videos started airing regularly on VH-1 and here was this slightly geeky, red-headed white dude from England singing like a genuine child of Motown.

At the same time that Rick Astley was making noise on the charts, so was a fellow called Grayson Hugh, another white singer who possessed decidedly black vocal chops. Listening to "Talk It Over," Hugh's only hit record, one could hear shades of Sam Cooke, Otis Redding, and Smokey Robinson, blended with the blue-eyed soul of Rod Stewart and Michael Bolton.

It's rather surprising that "Talk It Over" never climbed higher than #19 and only spent a modest eight weeks in the Top 40, as this was a solid, well-constructed piece of pop. The song featured a thick, chugging bass line, the kind of deep groove that beautifully anchored the track from start to finish. Layered over this memorable bass line were Grayson Hugh's emotive, heartfelt lead vocals, all complemented by some of the smoothest, sweetest background harmonies ever laid down on wax. An amalgamation of Dan Hartman's "I Can Dream About You," The Isley Brothers' "This Old Heart of Mine (Is Weak for You)," and Sam Cooke's "A Change Is Gonna Come," "Talk It Over" was easily among the best singles released during the 1980s.

It's fair, yet unfortunate, to say that Grayson Hugh is scarcely recalled today. His only two albums, 1988's *Blind to Reason* and *Road to Freedom* from 1992, are out of print, and his Top 20 charter from '89 has virtually vanished from the FM airwaves, seldom even surfacing on *Saturday Night at the 80s*–type shows. About the only place you'll find "Talk It Over" nowadays is on compilation CDs such as *Sexy Soul, Living in the Eighties, Vol. 2,* and *Pretty Girls, Everywhere: Beach Classics, Vol. 1.*

By the way, a year before Grayson Hugh enjoyed his success with "Talk It Over," Olivia Newton-John issued an album called *The Rumour,* the third cut on which was "Can't We Talk It Over in Bed"— same song, slightly different title. ONJ's take on the Sandy Linzer/ Irwin Levine–penned tune failed to dent the charts.

Brent's Two Cents: Curiously, many of the really good one-hitters from the late 80s have been lost in the shuffle over the years. Songs like "The Promise" by When in Rome, Gregory Abbott's "Shake You Down," "Waiting for a Star to Fall" by Boy Meets Girl, Danny Wilson's "Mary's Prayer," "Shattered Dreams" by Johnny Hates Jazz, "Breakout" by Swing Out Sister, and, naturally, Grayson Hugh's "Talk It Over" were all terrific tunes that have been largely forgotten.

Ironically, though, a boatload of inferior one-hit wonders from the early 80s are very much remembered today, records like "Mickey" by Toni Basil, Musical Youth's "Pass the Dutchie," "Puttin' on the Ritz" by Taco, and Charlene's "I've Never Been to Me." Well, as they say in Brooklyn: Go figure!

#71

"Missing" by Everything But the Girl, 1995

And I miss you
Like the deserts miss the rain

Peaked nationally at #2
Lead singer: Tracey Thorn
Written by Tracey Thorn and Ben Watt

"In the summer of 1992, on the eve of an American tour, Ben Watt, one half of the *Billboard*-topping pop duo Everything But the Girl, was taken to a London hospital complaining of chest pains. He didn't leave for two and a half months." That's what it said on the back cover of *Patient: The True Story of a Rare Illness,* Ben Watt's book about his successful battle against a life-threatening disease known as Churg-Strauss Syndrome.

Well, it certainly wasn't an easy road; however, Watt and his wife, Tracey Thorn, the British couple known as Everything But the Girl, not only managed to weather an extremely trying period, but they also found the energy and creativity to wax what was to become, with the help of a fellow named Todd Terry, one of the most memorable tracks of the mid-90s.

Thirty-seven weeks is more than nine full months, and that's how long "Missing" spent in the Top 40. In fact, of all the 101 songs featured on our tour of the best one-hit wonders, with the exception of Duncan Sheik's "Barely Breathing," none enjoyed a longer chart run than Everything But the Girl's lone hit single.

"Missing" first appeared on a 1994 album called *Amplified Heart.* Interestingly, though, this was not the version that received such massive radio play. No, it was actually a 1995 remix by the aforementioned Todd Terry, a New York producer, that became the almost unheard of 37-week Top 40 juggernaut. Terry's re-fashioning of the tune, dubbed the Todd Terry Club Mix, laid on a heavy dance/techno beat, a sound that broke through the clutter on the FM dial, and provided a refreshing change of pace to wimpy fluff like Celine Dion's "Because You Loved Me" and "Have You Ever Really Loved a Woman?" by Bryan Adams.

In listening to the original "Missing" next to the remix, you immediately notice that the former is far darker and more atmospheric than the latter. But it was the Todd Terry Club Mix with its pulsating grooves that really caught America's collective ear. Indeed, the Terry

---

Regarding the strange name Tracey Thorn and Ben Watt adopted for their group, Everything But the Girl, one story has it that a store in Hull, England, was holding a massive going-out-of-business sale, a complete selling-to-the-bare-walls liquidation where customers were encouraged to make an offer on "everything but the girl." The "girl" in this case referred to the young lady behind the cash register.

Other one-hitters with odd monikers include: Bent Fabric ("Alley Cat"), Timbuk 3 ("The Future's So Bright, I Gotta Wear Shades"), Frankie Goes to Hollywood ("Relax"), Living in a Box ("Living in a Box"), and Brighter Side of Darkness ("Love Jones").

remix quickly became a 90s compilation staple, appearing on numerous collections, including *Ultimate Dance Party 1997, Simply the Best Radio Hits,* and *The Best of Dance Mix USA.*

To date, Everything But the Girl has issued more than a dozen compact discs, the latest being 2001's *Back to Mine,* and over the course of their 20-year recording career the duo has explored every genre from jazz to straight-ahead pop to dance to trip-hop to jungle to rap to deep house to electronica to cocktail.

#70

"Shake You Down" by Gregory Abbott, 1986

You read my mind, you know you did
Girl, I wanna shake you down

Peaked nationally at #1
Lead singer: Gregory Abbott
Written by Gregory Abbott

"Shake You Down" was an unusual single in that it was embraced by an exceptionally wide variety of radio formats. For example, take stations in a city like San Francisco: In its waning days as a Top 40 giant on the AM dial, KFRC was spinning Gregory Abbott's record, and just down the street, the song was also being played on KBLX, the Bay Area's so-called Quiet Storm station. KYUU and K-101, the market's Contemporary Hit Radio powerhouses, were airing "Shake You Down," too. And, naturally, KSOL, the city's Urban outlet, gave Abbott's tune its due as well. AM stations. FM stations. White audiences. Black audiences. Mainstream pop lovers. R&B lovers. This #1 smash was everywhere, appealing to everybody.

The genius of "Shake You Down" was the manner in which it deftly infused a commercial pop flavor into what was, at its core, a deeply soulful rhythm and blues record. This blend of soul and pop put Abbott in the company of artists like DeBarge, Atlantic Starr, The Commodores, and Anita Baker. Yet, unlike those other acts, Gregory Abbott managed to chart only once, which had to be disappointing to the singer and songwriter. Four albums starting back in 1986, just one Top 40 success.

In listening to Abbott's body of work, you certainly hear a smooth, confident sound, but only "Shake You Down" possesses a memorable musical hook, that all-important, hard-to-come-by element that has always separated a merely *good* song from a *hit* song. You get the impression that he's been more concerned with waxing polished, professional tracks than loosening up a bit, letting go, and perhaps creating something a little rawer, or even quirkier, that might really grab the listener's ears.

By the way, Gregory Abbott, who was born in Manhattan in 1954,

---

1986, the year Gregory Abbott and his "Shake You Down" burst onto the pop charts, was an active 12 months for one-hit wonders. Here is a roll call of some of the more obscure acts whose lone Top 40 single came in '86: Communards ("Don't Leave Me This Way"), Chico DeBarge ("Talk to Me"), Device ("Hanging on a Heart Attack"), Double ("Captain of Her Heart"), Honeymoon Suite ("Feel It Again"), Oran "Juice" Jones ("The Rain"), Jeff Lorber ("Facts of Love"), Marilyn Martin ("Night Moves"), Nancy Martinez ("For Tonight"), Models ("Out of Mind Out of Sight"), Sly Fox ("Let's Go All the Way"), Robert Tepper ("No Easy Way Out"), and Timex Social Club ("Rumors").

Hats off and major bonus points to anyone who recalls Device, Honeymoon Suite, or Nancy Martinez, because those artists and their songs are definitely back-of-the-rack one-hitters.

was briefly married to Freda Payne, the singer from Detroit who en-joyed three Top 40 hits in the very early 70s: "Band of Gold," "Deeper & Deeper," and "Bring the Boys Home." Abbott and Payne had one child together, Gregory Abbott, Jr.

Shake You Down, the album from '86 that spawned Abbott's mon-ster single, is still in print. "Shake You Down" is also available on any number of compilation CDs, including *Quiet Storm Memories, Body + Soul: Between the Sheets,* and *The Most Beautiful Soul Album on Earth.*

#69

"I Can Help" by Billy Swan, 1974

It would sure do me good to do you good
Let me help!

Peaked nationally at #1
Lead singer: Billy Swan
Written by Billy Swan

Cape Girardeau, Missouri, gave us Rush Limbaugh, the conservative talk-show host. This city of 35,000, hard by the banks of the Mississippi River, also produced Billy Swan, a colorful one-hitter who enjoyed a #1 smash at the end of 1974.

Long before "I Can Help," Swan penned a song called "Lover Please," which the late Clyde McPhatter of Drifters fame carried all the way to #7 back in 1962. It took another dozen years for the Missourian to re-connect with the Top 40.

There's an old saying in the recording industry: "If it's in the grooves, it moves," the word "moves" meaning "sells." That certainly applied to "I Can Help." Here was a tune that had no business going all the way to the top of the pop world insofar as the record was, at its heart, rockabilly. And, let's face it, in terms of mainstream popularity, rockabilly peaked in the mid-50s with the likes of Gene Vincent, Jerry Lee Lewis, Carl "Blue Suede Shoes" Perkins, and, naturally, The King, Elvis Presley. So, it came as a surprise, in the mid-70s, to witness "I Can Help" zoom up the charts. This single just plain had the right stuff in the grooves, so it moved beautifully.

The curious thing about Swan's track is just how familiar it sounded from the very first listen, as if it were a song that had been around forever, a tune everyone knew by heart and loved singing along to. The twangy, countrified lead vocal, the bouncy, toe-tapping beat—the entire package was fun, comforting and, again, eminently *familiar.*

Interestingly, a lot of AM listeners initially thought "I Can Help" was a Ringo Starr record. Now, you might be thinking to yourself, "C'mon, you mean to tell me that folks were actually mistaking an American rockabilly singer with an English dude who sang with a thick Liverpudlian accent?!" Granted, at first blush, it seems crazy, but if you check out the former Beatle on numbers like "Oh My My," "You're Sixteen," and "It Don't Come Easy," songs with a definite Memphis and Nashville vibe, it's not so hard to understand why some confused Swan with Starr.

At a time when people still bought 45s, the "I Can Help" single flew

Billy Swan's "I Can Help" is part of a compilation CD called *AM Gold: Top 40 Treasures.* This album's title is an excellent reminder that the AM radio dial was, for a good quarter-century, from, say, 1955 to 1980, the place where millions of listeners turned every day for their fill of pop/rock music. Admittedly, the sound could be tinny and rife with static, but no one seemed to mind. AM powerhouses like WQXI in Atlanta, WTKQ (13Q) in Pittsburgh, and Seattle's KJR were spinning our favorite songs, and that's all that really mattered.

off the shelves. In fact, worldwide, Billy Swan sold more than five million copies of his smash. "If it's in the grooves, it moves." By the way, in recent years, "I Can Help", has become a real favorite of national television advertisers, and you might recall its use in spots peddling everything from Texaco gasoline to videos at Blockbuster.

Along with Marlu, his wife of more than 30 years, Billy Swan lives in Southern California's San Fernando Valley. The couple has two grown daughters, Planet and Sierra.

#68

"Wicked Game" by Chris Isaak, 1991

I never dreamed that I'd love somebody like you
And I never dreamed that I'd lose somebody like you

Peaked nationally at #6
Lead singer: Chris Isaak
Written by Chris Isaak

As he stood there, shaking hands, rocking back and forth to the sound of his own music, periodically messing with his hair, he was a brash young cross between Elvis and Robert Mitchum.
—MICHAEL GOLDBERG'S DESCRIPTION OF CHRIS ISAAK IN THE *SAN FRANCISCO EXAMINER*, APRIL 6, 1986

Shot in atmospheric black and white on the island of Hawaii, the "Wicked Game" video oozed sexuality. From the fast-moving clouds to the crashing Pacific waves to the barely clothed young babe with bee-stung lips, the watchword for a solid four minutes was, plain and simply, "sex." It made you want to yell at the TV screen, "Hey, you two, get a room already!" Indeed, the proceedings resembled nothing so much as a piece of soft-core porn, a video that definitely held the attention of all the 14- and 15-year-old *Beavis & Butt-head* fans back in the winter of '91.

"Wicked Game" appeared on 1989's *Heart Shaped World,* Isaak's third album. However, don't search for the song on the 1989 charts, because you won't find it. It took "Wicked Game's" exposure in *Wild at Heart,* the 1990 David Lynch film starring Laura Dern and Nicolas Cage, to propel the record into the Top 40, where it spent three months, peaking at #6.

From the opening note, "Wicked Game" has *smash single* written all over it, which is why it's astonishing that the tune didn't immediately take flight in the late 80s upon its initial release. The best way to describe this song is Roy Orbison meets ultra-slick, late-twentieth-century production values. Isaak's voice is, by turns, smooth and warbly, just like Orbison's.

To date, Chris Isaak has released eight CDs, all of which remain in print. His sound on these releases slides from Roy Orbison ("Wicked Game" and "Think of Tomorrow") to early Elvis ("Forever Blue") to George Thorogood ("Baby Did a Bad Bad Thing"). Although his style follows in the footsteps of wildly popular artists, apart from "Wicked Game," Isaak's music has proven too refined and sophisticated for commercial radio. It's strange, but in many ways this singer and guitarist from Stockton, California, has been almost too successful in blending disparate musical genres, to the extent that listeners go away unsatisfied. For example, Chris Isaak whips up a tasty batch of rockabilly, but not enough to please, say, a Stray Cats fan. He lays on a touch of country, but Lyle Lovett aficionados want even more. And the mainstream popsters who were clamoring for non-stop Whitney Houston, Phil Collins, and Mariah Carey, well, Isaak's offerings were too twangy, too country.

In addition to making records, Isaak has actively pursued an acting career over the years. He's appeared in movies such as *Married to the Mob, Little Buddha, That Thing You Do!,* and *The Silence of the*

Lambs. And, of course, in 2001, Showtime premiered *The Chris Isaak Show,* a sitcom based loosely on the singer's own life as a performer.

Brent's Two Cents: In 1990, *People* magazine dubbed Chris Isaak one of its "50 Most Beautiful People," and with good reason. Just look at his album covers (especially *Silvertone*). The man is channeling Elvis Presley circa 1957.

#67

"(Just Like) Romeo & Juliet" by The Reflections, 1964

Our love's gonna be written down in history
Ah, just like Romeo and Juliet

Peaked nationally at #6
Lead singer: Tony Micale
Written by Freddie Gorman and Bob Hamilton

Spring, 1964. The country is still reeling in the aftermath of Friday, November 22, 1963, the day John F. Kennedy was assassinated in Dallas. However, millions of Americans are finding much-needed diversion and solace in pop music, and The Reflections, a group out of the western suburbs of Detroit, are rocketing up the charts with a bouncy number called "(Just Like) Romeo & Juliet."

The Reflections were composed of Danny Bennie, Phil Castrodale, Johnny Dean, Tony Micale, and Ray Steinberg, all of whom sang on "Romeo & Juliet," with Micale leading the vocal charge. And, indeed, it was Tony Micale's clear, energetic tenor that really carried this number, as his voice jumped right off the platter.

"(Just Like) Romeo & Juliet" appeared on an album of the same name, and when the song was issued as a single, it sold four million copies, propelling it to #6. Although The Reflections only issued one LP, some 40 years later their smash hit continues to turn up on compilations like *60's Sock Hop, Good Time Gold,* and *1964—The Beat Goes On.* Surprisingly, the runaway success of "Romeo & Juliet" failed to pave the way for follow-up releases such as "Poor Man's Son," "Like Columbus Did," and "Shabby Little Hut," as none of these tunes reached the Top 40. However, because The Reflections incorporated more than a little doo-wop into their sound, maybe the group would have fared better in the late 50s as opposed to the dawning of the British Invasion. Sometimes a talented act just finds itself peddling a particular brand of music at a rather unreceptive time, and this, unfortunately, was the case with Messrs. Bennie, Castrodale, Dean, Micale, and Steinberg.

During the mid-60s, at the height of their popularity, The Reflections were guests on television's *Shindig, Hullabaloo,* and *American Bandstand.* They also did a turn in *Winter-a-Go-Go,* a long-forgotten movie from '65 that was set at a ski lodge. During that same period, the band also performed throughout the country as part of "Dick Clark's Caravan of Stars." Fast forward a quarter-century and—certainly not on the strength of their exposure in *Winter-a-Go-Go*—the outfit was inducted into Michigan's Rock 'n' Roll Hall of Fame.

Today, Tony Micale and Johnny Dean, two of the original Reflections, are singing with Gary Banovetz, Joey Finazzo, and Bernie Turnbull, the three of whom were members of a group called The Larados.

Many pop/rock fans think that Detroit's musical history begins and ends with the Motown label. Well, obviously, the likes of Marvin Gaye, Diana Ross, The Four Tops, Smokey Robinson, and Martha & the Vandellas are legendary acts spawned from the 313 area code, but let's not forget Ted "The Motor City Madman" Nugent, Mitch Ryder, Bob Seger, Glenn Frey, as well as a woman—who's been known to sell a record or two—by the name of Madonna.

These five doo-woppers, all now in their 60s, keep an active schedule, regularly staging shows under The Reflections banner at Detroit-area venues like Motor City Casino, Hiawatha Racetrack, and The Capital Theatre in Windsor, Ontario.

#66

"Waiting for a Star to Fall" by Boy Meets Girl, 1988

Trying to catch your heart is like trying to catch a
*   star*
So many people love you, baby, that must be what
*   you are*

Peaked nationally at #5
Lead singer: George Merrill
Written by Shannon Rubicam and George Merrill

"Waiting for a Star to Fall" was just solid, well-crafted late-80s pop, and small wonder, considering that it was written by Shannon Rubicam and George Merrill, the same pair who penned smashes for Whitney Houston like "How Will I Know" and "I Wanna Dance with Somebody (Who Loves Me)." The duo also wrote songs for Paul Young, Bette Midler, and Deniece "Let's Hear It for the Boy" Williams.

Boy Meets Girl was the name adopted by Rubicam and Merrill when this couple from Seattle decided to wax their own records back in 1985. All told, they issued three albums: *Boy Meets Girl, Reel Life,* and *New Dream,* with "Waiting for a Star to Fall" coming off 1988's *Reel Life.*

Shannon Rubicam and George Merrill's Top 5 track, which spent an impressive four months on the charts, possessed a bright, clean energy, a sound that really stood out from the mellower, more down-tempo fare of the day, tunes like "Kokomo" by The Beach Boys and "Hold On to the Nights" by Richard Marx. The best part of "Waiting for a Star to Fall" was the manner in which the single effectively built up the musical tension and then quickly released it, a device employed by many professional songwriters and worked to perfection by the team of Rubicam and Merrill.

Even though none of Boy Meets Girl's compact discs remains in print, "Waiting for a Star to Fall" is readily available on more than a dozen compilations, including *Entertainment Weekly: The Greatest Hits 1988, Rock & Roll Relix: 1980–1989,* and *Do You Love Me? All-Time Best Love Songs.* The song also appeared on the *Three Men and a Baby* soundtrack.

By the way, in the spring of 1985, a full three years before earning a #5 spot on the Top 40, Boy Meets Girl spent a solitary week at #39 with a song called "Oh Girl." A tune that peaks at #39 simply isn't a bona fide hit record, so let's not go crazy and refer to "Oh Girl" as the duo's second hit.

Radio stations spin one-hit wonders. Television stations air one-hit wonder videos. And websites write about them. Here are two interesting musings from cyberspace:

"I dare anybody to walk up to Lou [Reed], walking around the East Village, and call him a 'one-hit wonder.'"
—Rick Levin, writing on thestranger.com, bemoaning the fact that Lou "Walk on the Wild Side" Reed is technically a one-hitter

"The one-hit wonder—funny how they often linger longer in the subconscious than the multiple-hit bores."
—cluas.com, Ireland's self-proclaimed "most trafficked music webzine"

In 2000, Shannon Rubicam and George Merrill divorced after more than a decade of marriage. The scuttlebutt within the music biz is that they recorded several songs inspired by their break-up, but this material has apparently never surfaced.

#65

"Life Is a Highway" by Tom Cochrane, 1992

Life is a highway
I want to ride it all night long

Peaked nationally at #6
Lead singer: Tom Cochrane
Written by Tom Cochrane

What do Bruce Cockburn ("Wondering Where the Lions Are"), Kon Kan ("I Beg Your Pardon"), Byron MacGregor ("Americans"), and Tom Cochrane, the subject at hand, have in common? Well, in addition to being one-hit wonders, each of these acts hailed from Canada.

Lynn Lake is 650 miles north of Winnipeg, Manitoba, which is just another way of saying that some 50 years ago Tom Cochrane was born in the middle of nowhere. It was fortuitous for Cochrane that by the 1960s his mother and father, Violet and Tuck, had moved the family to Etobicoke, Ontario, a suburb of Toronto. Indeed, by the time he'd reached his early 20s, the singer and guitarist was grinding out a living playing at bars and coffeehouses throughout The Big Smoke.

So, when the summer of '92 rolled around and "Life Is a Highway" shot up the charts, it must have amazed, and somewhat annoyed, Tom Cochrane that American disk jockeys were breathlessly telling their listeners about this "terrific new talent from Canada." Yeah, some "new" talent—Cochrane had only been active in the music business for a mere 20-plus years, a genuine overnight success.

"Life Is a Highway," which spent an impressive five months in the Top 40, was just solid, good-time rock 'n' roll. Nothing fancy, no gimmicks or frills. And Cochrane's ballsy, high-energy record came at the perfect time, as the airwaves were being enervated by artists such as Boyz II Men ("End of the Road"), Billy Ray Cyrus ("Achy Breaky Heart"), Peabo Bryson ("Beauty and the Beast"), and TLC ("Baby-Baby-Baby").

Mad Mad World was the album that spawned Tom Cochrane's #6 song, and since then "Life Is a Highway" has appeared on CD collections like *Living in the '90s, To the Extreme,* and *Modern Rock Superstars of the 90s.*

During the 1980s, Cochrane fronted an outfit called Red Rider, a band that enjoyed a tremendous following in their native Canada, scoring a string of hit singles in The Great White North, including "Lunatic Fringe," "Boy Inside the Man," and "Power (Strength in Numbers)." As a solo act, "Life Is a Highway" notwithstanding, Cochrane has never equaled his success as part of Red Rider.

Today, more than a decade after his moment in the Top 10 spotlight, Tom Cochrane has all but vanished from the American pop music radar. Apart from the odd spin during a "Totally 90s Weekend," "Life Is a Highway" is totally M.I.A. from the FM dial nowadays. However, north of the border, Cochrane continues releasing CDs and gigging at venues from the Rock & Roll Warehouse in St. John, New Brunswick, to the Dawson Creek Arena in British Columbia.

Brent's Two Cents: "Life Is a Highway" is one of those tunes that sounds great in a convertible with the top down, cranked to full volume. That being said, there's always been a certain unsatisfying something about Cochrane's hit single. It's as if the song could have been even better with just a bit more imagination and effort. Perhaps Dave DiMartino, writing in *Entertainment Weekly,* hit the nail on the head when he penned the following about Tom Cochrane's *Mad Mad World* LP, off which "Life Is a Highway" was culled: "[It's] well crafted, extremely soulless radio fodder, a clever replica of music that wasn't even that interesting in the first place."

#64

"Dirty Water" by The Standells, 1966

That's where you'll find me
Along with lovers, fuggers, and thieves

Peaked nationally at #11
Lead singer: Dick Dodd
Written by Ed Cobb

Inasmuch as their lone hit was all about their love of the city on the Charles River, many AM listeners back in the summer of '66 assumed The Standells were from Boston. Well, they weren't. Actually, the band hailed from Los Angeles. Yep, Southern Californians singing the praises of Beantown.

The Standells were composed of Dick Dodd, Gary Lane, Larry Tamblyn (brother of actor Russ Tamblyn, best known for playing "Riff" in the film version of *West Side Story*), and Tony Valentino. Guys named Dave Burke, John Fleck, and Gary Leeds held membership in later incarnations of the group, but Messrs. Dodd, Lane, Tamblyn, and Valentino constituted the original line-up, the quartet that went into the studio and put "Dirty Water" down on wax.

If you liked an early Rolling Stones track called "The Last Time" off the *Out of Our Heads* LP from 1965, then a year later you probably also enjoyed The Standells' "Dirty Water," the sound of which, especially the introduction, was essentially a pastiche of The Stones' number. On the other hand, you might have found "Dirty Water" to be a complete filching of "The Last Time," in which case . . . well, you get the idea.

To this day, Dick Dodd's lead vocals on "Dirty Water" rank among the most memorable in pop/rock history. Dodd sang, casually talked, growled, shrieked, and mumbled his way through the tune. His style was a sonic mishmash of Mick Jagger, John Lee Hooker, and Jack Ely, the singer on The Kingsmen's 1963 classic "Louie, Louie." And for the record's less-than-three-minute duration, it all came together marvelously.

Placing "Dirty Water" into a specific rock 'n' roll sub-genre has always been a fascinating parlor game among fans of mid-60s music. Some call the song garage rock. Others, blues rock. Or, how about frat rock? There is even the camp that insists "Dirty Water" is proto punk rock, which, interestingly enough, might very well be the most accurate categorization of them all. Indeed, consider the following blurb taken from the liner notes of *The Best of The Standells:* "There's a wealth of current punk bands with names like The Unclaimed, Chesterfield Kings, Barracudas, Pandoras, and more who either perform Standells songs, or are in other ways quite clearly influenced by them."

Between 1964 and 1967, The Standells released six albums: *Live and Out of Sight, Standells Live at P.J.'s, Dirty Water, Why Pick on Me,*

Virtually every one-hit single featured on our musical tour has eventually found its way onto numerous compilation CDs, and "Dirty Water" is no exception. Check out these very colorfully named collections that contain The Standells' #11 hit: *Frat Rock!, Garage Band Classics, Music to Watch Cartoons By,* and *Nuggets From Nuggets: Choice Artyfacts from the First Psychedelic Era.* An album called *Music to Watch Cartoons By?* You simply can't top that for a title.

Hot Ones, and *Try It.* For years, none of these LPs was available on compact disc. However, in 2002, a label called Big Beat UK packaged *Dirty Water* together with *Why Pick on Me,* releasing it on a single CD. Big Beat UK also did the same with *Hot Ones* and *Try It,* issuing those as a combo disc.

#63

"Whip It" by Devo, 1980

Crack that whip
Give the past the slip

Peaked nationally at #14
Lead singer: Mark Mothersbaugh
Written by Jerry Casale and Mark Mothersbaugh

To call the "Whip It" video "strange" is to understate the case. A better description would be "bizarre and surreal." Name another clip that features: 1) a log cabin occupied by an apron-clad Italian mama and a mysterious cross-eyed Asian woman; 2) model-gorgeous cowboys and cowgirls leaning against a wooden fence, sipping Budweiser from the can; and 3) a lead singer wearing a red flowerpot on his head, wielding a black whip.

Was "Whip It" a great song? Well, that point is highly debatable. However, there is no arguing that Devo's only Top 40 single was extremely memorable. Indeed, it would be hard to find a person between the ages of, say, 30 and 50 who does not have a vivid recollection of "Whip It." In addition to an unforgettable video, the tune itself possessed a mesmerizing techno beat and robotic vocals, the kind of unusual track that made listeners want to bop their heads and break into a herky-jerky dance.

Getting a handle on Devo's overall sound has never been an easy matter. By some measures, they were purveyors of synth pop, putting them in the same boat with the likes of Gary Numan ("Cars"), Human League ("[Keep Feeling] Fascination"), Eurythmics ("Sweet Dreams [Are Made of This]"), and Soft Cell ("Tainted Love"). But somehow, the synth pop label doesn't exactly fit Devo. Of course, at times, the outfit from Akron, Ohio, was also painted with the punk brush. However, viewing Devo in the same light as American punks such as The Ramones, Dead Kennedys, and Television, well, that never really worked, either. So, maybe the "Whip It" guys were just plain late 70s/early 80s New Wavers, right? Yet, lumping Devo together with The Knack ("My Sharona" and "Good Girls Don't"), Elvis Costello ("Alison"), and Cheap Trick ("I Want You to Want Me") doesn't make all that much sense.

In actual fact, more than anything else, Devo was a piece of experimental performance art, a combination of avant-garde dress and music layered on top of an unorthodox world view. The band's members—Bob Casale, Jerry Casale, Bob Mothersbaugh, Mark Mothersbaugh, and Alan Myers—subscribed to the unconventional idea that mankind was on a slow, inevitable slide backward, a sort of devolution, if you will. This theory of devolution was, naturally, the inspiration for the group's name, Devo.

Apart from "Whip It," Devo's songs were, quite simply, too far out and counter-culture for mainstream radio, which is why the likes of "Freedom of Choice," "Jocko Homo," and "Mongoloid" never cracked the Top 40.

Brent's Two Cents: Devo's album covers were both wacky and brilliant. Take *Freedom of Choice,* the LP that spawned "Whip It." Here were the guys all decked out in black T-shirts, black leather jackets, topped off, of course, by their trademark plastic flowerpot hats. Each member of the group was staring straight ahead, looking totally dispassionate.

Then, there was the *Q: Are We Not Men? A: We Are Devo!* album from 1978. This cover featured a drawing of a golf ball, superimposed over which was the image of a clean-cut, *uber*-WASP very much re-sembling J.R. "Bob" Dobbs of Church of the SubGenius fame.

By the way, in 2002, "Whip It" was used in a television spot for Gateway, the personal computer giant. Here was the subversive Devo, the outfit that saw technology turning humans into robots, and 22 years later their hit single was being pressed into service to sing the praises of high technology—a delicious irony.

#62

"I Know" by Dionne Farris, 1995

I know what you're doing—yeah, yeah
I know why you dial my number

Peaked nationally at #4
Lead singer: Dionne Farris
Written by Milton Davis and William Duvall

Remember the big hit Journey had in the winter of 1982 with "Open Arms"? While Steve Perry & Co. eventually kicked things into high gear, the proceedings started rather gently and deliberately with a soft, tinkling piano, allowing the tune to slowly unfold and gather steam. This let-the-energy-gradually-build approach suited a song like "Open Arms" perfectly. Now, the current stop on our one-hit wonder tour, "I Know" by Dionne Farris, well, this was a number that took a completely different tack, staging a sonic assault right from the get-go. *Boom!* No pussy-footing around, no warming to the task at hand—"I Know" got right down to business.

Dionne Farris's single spent an amazing 29 weeks on the charts. Listeners simply did not tire of this record. Think about it for a mo-ment—29 solid weeks. That's more than seven months as a staple on the FM airwaves. That's two full months longer than one-hitter

Debby Boone's "You Light Up My Life," which was a mega success by any measure. Or, consider this: The Beatles' "Hey Jude" spent 10 fewer weeks in the Top 40 than Dionne Farris's "I Know."

Wild Seed—Wild Flower was the name of the album that yielded "I Know." In listening to other cuts from this LP, it's obvious that Farris had talent; however, her music, apart from her Top 5 smash, lacked energy and direction. For example, a track like "Stop to Think" just rambled. There was plenty of moaning in the background, but where was the necessary pop hook? Then there was "Food for Thought," which was plodding and ponderous to the point of sounding like a dirge. Granted, not every song needs to brim with vigor to be successful, yet a certain drive, spark, and focus should be a part of every tune to save it from meandering aimlessly.

In addition to *Wild Seed—Wild Flower,* which is still in print, "I Know" is available as part of compilations such as *Billboard Top Hits: 1995, Unstoppable 90's—Urban Jams,* and *Intimate Portrait: Women with Soul,* the latter of which was released on the Lifetime Television label.

Eight years after zooming all the way to #4 and enjoying that remarkable run of 29 weeks in the Top 40, Dionne Farris is a forgotten figure, a genuine one-hit wonder. After having such a monster hit with "I Know," it's baffling that the brass over at Sony Music didn't immediately hustle Farris back into the studio to start crafting a follow-up album in hopes of keeping the momentum going.

By the way, before launching a solo career, Farris did some recording with Arrested Development, the rappers out of Atlanta. If you listen to the song called "Tennessee," which Arrested Development landed at #6 in 1992, you can hear Dionne Farris singing between the rap. Not surprisingly, after doing well with "Tennessee," the singer decided to strike out on her own. Arrested Development pressed on after Farris's departure, managing to score two more hit singles: "People Everyday," a #8 record in the fall of '92, and "Mr. Wendal," which climbed to #6 in early 1993. By the end of the 90s, though, both Dionne Farris and Arrested Development had totally fallen off the musical radar screen.

#61

"Pump Up the Volume" by M/A/R/R/S, 1988

Put the needle on the record
When the drum beats go like this

Peaked nationally at #13
Lead singer: Various rap samples, including Eric B. &
     Rakim
Written by Martyn Young

"Pump Up the Volume" was a musical hodge-podge, borrowing freely from a variety of styles, including pop, rap, funk, trance, dance, house, industrial, electronica, and even jungle. And it all came together marvelously.

M/A/R/R/S was composed of Alex Ayuli, Rudy Tambala, Martyn Young, and Steve Young. Ayuli and Tambala first made their mark with an outfit from London's East End called AR Kane. Four albums were issued under the AR Kane banner, all of which featured liberal doses of sampling and feedback. As for brothers Martyn and Steve Young, they came to M/A/R/R/S from Colourbox, a band also out of London that specialized in a sort of acid-dance sound.

The genius of "Pump Up the Volume" is the manner in which it transports the listener so seamlessly and satisfyingly among such disparate sonic landscapes. One moment you're deep within a trance vibe, while the next you're in the middle of an energetic rap, and then, before you know it, the record blasts your ears off on a journey to the far reaches of a planet named Electronica. The effect is positively magical.

During its brief existence, M/A/R/R/S never released a full-blown album, so "Pump Up the Volume" was put out on the Atlantic label as a so-called EP, an extended play single. The EP featured several different versions of the track. Not surprisingly, as the song drips with atmosphere, "Pump Up the Volume" has been used effectively in movies such as *Bright Lights, Big City* and *American Pyscho*. The tune was also heard in *My Stepmother Is an Alien*; indeed, it was the best part of that otherwise forgettable film from '88 starring Kim Basinger, Dan Aykroyd, and Jon Lovitz.

M/A/R/R/S's #13 hit has also been packaged as part of a slew of compilation CDs, including *Greatest Sports Rock and Jams, Megadance into the 90's,* as well as *More of Club Mix's Biggest Jams.*

Regrettably, at least from the perspective of people who enjoy innovative pop, just as Messrs. Ayuli, Tambala, Young, and Young were witnessing their "Pump Up the Volume" achieve worldwide success, they decided to pack it in. There would be no M/A/R/R/S follow-up. One can only imagine the gloom over at Atlantic Records, as they saw a quartet of talented Londoners—surefire money makers!—voluntarily relegate themselves to one-hit wonderdom.

To this day, precisely why the group folded remains somewhat of a mystery. Vague terms like "disputes over money" and "creative differences" have been offered up as possible explanations for the demise, but perhaps the principals were just burned out from making music in general. Consider, for example, Alex Ayuli. In the wake of M/A/R/R/S, he left England with his wife and headed to Northern California, where he spent a fair bit of time indulging a hobby of his, the study of Chinese furniture. When a musician would rather *contemplate Chinese furniture* than make million-selling records, well, then, breaking up his band probably was the logical decision.

The Mysteries Within was an album issued in 2001 by a group called Mars. In 1999, a compact disc entitled *Holding Hands @ 35,000 Ft.* was released on the Intersound label. The artist? Denison Marrs. Of course, Denison Marrs is not to be confused with the jazz drummer Jeff Marrs or the singer Christina Marrs.

#60

"Precious and Few"
by Climax, 1972

And if I can't find my way back home, it just wouldn't
*   be fair*
'Cause precious and few are the moments we two can
*   share*

Peaked nationally at #3
Lead singer: Sonny Geraci
Written by Walter Nims

"Precious and Few" is one of those rare songs that cuts a wide generational swath: Not only are you familiar with this tune, but so is your mother and even your grandmother. Interestingly, though, for a record that is so well known, nobody can ever seem to correctly recall the name of the artist that launched it into the Top 5. "Oh, sure, 'Precious and Few,' I remember that one. It was done by . . . umm, let's see, wait a minute, Climax Blues Band, right?" Well, actually, no, Climax Blues Band was a group from England known for "Couldn't Get It Right" and "I Love You."

Climax was formed in 1971 in Southern California by Sonny Geraci, Robert Neilson, Walter Nims, Virgil Weber, and Steve York. Geraci, the driving force behind the band and lead vocalist on "Precious and Few," had known success in the 60s as part of The Outsiders, a group from Cleveland, Ohio, that in 1966 alone scored four Top 40 hits: "Time Won't Let Me," "Girl in Love," "Respectable," and "Help Me Girl."

"Precious and Few" became such a smash because it was a direct, beautifully crafted love song along the lines of "(They Long to Be) Close to You" by The Carpenters and Bread's "Everything I Own," a number that was unabashedly sentimental. And, of course, Sonny

Geraci's voice fit the material to a tee: sincere and sweet, without lapsing into sappiness, all set against lush, but not overpowering, instrumentals.

Climax's lone hit came off an album on the Rocky Road label simply called *Climax*; in fact, it was the group's only LP, and, not surprisingly, it's long out of print. However, "Precious and Few" is still very much available, indeed, more than 50 compilation CDs feature the tune, among them *Rock 'n' Roll Relix 1972–1973, The Seventies Generation: 1972,* and *Chart Toppers: Romantic Hits of the 70s.*

After "Precious and Few" spent three months in the Top 40, Climax had no luck finding a successful follow-up. They released a single called "Life and Breath," but it ran out of steam at #52. The band also recorded "Rock and Roll Heaven," a song written by Alan "Undercover Angel" O'Day and Johnny Stevenson, a guy who had played keyboards on several Climax cuts. This effort fizzled, too. Of course, it had to be rather painful for Geraci & Co. to witness another act, The Righteous Brothers, ride their own version of "Rock and Roll Heaven" all the way to #3 in the summer of '74.

Sonny Geraci, a man who more than 30 years ago sang coast to coast on *Shindig, Hullabaloo, The Smothers Brothers Comedy Hour,* and *American Bandstand,* still entertains today, touring North America as star of "The Sonny Geraci Show." In addition, the singer has also issued *On the Verge* and *The Sonny Geraci Show Live!!,* two compact discs that are sold primarily through the Internet and at his concerts.

As for the other members of Climax, Steve York gigs regularly with bluesman Big John Dickerson, mostly at clubs in Minnesota. Virgil Weber is now a member of the Los Angeles–based Graham Dorsey Band. Sadly, Walter Nims, who penned "Precious and Few," died on April 6, 2000, of a stroke.

#59

"She Blinded Me with Science" by Thomas Dolby, 1983

She blinded me with science
And failed me in biology

Peaked nationally at #5
Lead singer: Thomas Dolby
Written by Thomas Dolby and Joseph Kerr

Dolby's first development under the aegis of his new
company [Dolby Laboratories] was called Dolby A-type
noise reduction. It was a sophisticated new form of
audio compression and expansion that dramatically re-
duced the background hiss inherent in professional tape
recording without discernible side effects on the material
being recorded.

—DOLBY.COM, DOLBY LABORATORIES, INC.'S
CORPORATE WEBSITE

Cool, huh? A one-hit wonder, the man who gave us the synth pop
classic "She Blinded Me with Science," was the inventor of Dolby
noise reduction. Well, actually, no, *that* would be a fellow by the
name of Ray Dolby, born in Portland, Oregon, in 1933. The subject at
hand is a Thomas Dolby, an Englishman who was born in Cairo,
Egypt, of all places, in 1958.

His given name was Thomas Robertson, and as a teenager he enjoyed mucking about and experimenting with gadgets of all sorts, especially sound and recording equipment, hence the Dolby moniker.
So it was, in 1982, that one Thomas Dolby released an album called
The Golden Age of Wireless, off which came the quirky track "She

Blinded Me with Science," a tune that rocketed to #5. By the way, it's interesting to note that this unqualified smash in America only reached as high as #31 in Britain, Dolby's home turf.

Featuring synthesizers, drum machines, and sterile, robotic vocals, "She Blinded Me with Science" epitomized the corner of the New Wave universe that seemed to prize a sleek style and electronic wizardry as much as, if not more than, genuine musical substance. "Cars" by Gary Numan, the Human League's "Don't You Want Me," "Whip It" by Devo, and Soft Cell's "Tainted Love"—all numbers cut from the same "She Blinded Me with Science" cloth. Incidentally, a guy named Mutt Lange can be heard doing backup vocals on this song. Lange, who made his bones producing acts like Foreigner and Def Leppard, is married to Shania Twain.

Of course, the most memorable part of Dolby's record was the contribution of the late Magnus Pike, an eccentric English television personality who hosted his own program in the 70s called *Don't Ask Me*. At random moments throughout the tune, Pike would intone with mock seriousness but a single word: "Science!" If you were listening to FM radio or watching MTV back in the spring of '83, two things were for certain: one, even though three-quarters of what Dexys Midnight Runners' lead vocalist Kevin Rowland was singing was utterly unintelligible, you were digging "Come on Eileen;" and two, Magnus Pike's cry of "Science!" was ringing in your ears several times per day.

Inasmuch as New Wave peaked in late 1983/early 1984, it comes as no surprise that Thomas Dolby had no luck scoring a Top 40 follow-up to "She Blinded Me with Science." A song with the enigmatic title of "Europa and the Pirate Twins," also taken from *The Golden Age of Wireless,* wheezed its way to #67, while Dolby's "Hyperactive," which was unusual for its blend of synthesizers and brass, stalled at #62.

Entering middle age, Thomas Dolby is still active in the music business. Indeed, in 2001 alone, he released a compact disc called *Forty*, which was recorded live, as well as *12x12,* a sort of "greatest hits" collection. As to the fact that Dolby had only one hit on this side of the Atlantic, well, let's just say that *12x12* probably sold better in Birmingham, U.K., than Birmingham, AL.

Brent's Two Cents: Since making its debut on August 1, 1981, MTV has aired tens of thousands of music videos, yet only a handful have achieved iconic status, "She Blinded Me with Science" being one of them. Thomas Dolby's video is set in the English countryside at the Home for Deranged Scientists, a handsome white mansion peopled by all manner of colorful characters, including Miss Sakamoto, the coy, sexy Japanese nurse, as well as a crazy-eyed elderly gent playing croquet with a pool cue. An unforgettable slice of 1980s pop culture, for sure.

#58

"I Love the Nightlife (Disco 'Round)" by Alicia Bridges, 1978

Please don't talk about love tonight
Your sweet talking won't make it right

Peaked nationally at #5
Lead singer: Alicia Bridges
Written by Susan Hutcheson and Alicia Bridges

Did you know that disco record sales were up 400% for the year ending 1976? If these trends continue...Aaay!"
—DISCO STU FROM A 1997 EPISODE OF *THE SIMPSONS*

The Hues Corporation was a group out of Los Angeles that scored a #1 smash in the summer of 1974 with "Rock the Boat." In fact, "Rock the Boat" is generally considered by musicologists to be the very first mainstream disco record, the song that launched an extremely memorable pop era. Eight years later, in 1982, a tune called "Love Is in Control (Finger on the Trigger)" by Donna Summer climbed to #10. That track, along with the likes of Michael Jackson's "Billie Jean" and "It's Raining Men" by The Weather Girls, brought down the curtain on disco.

1978, spilling into 1979, was disco's zenith. From Philadelphia to Phoenix, an entire nation boogied to "Night Fever" by the Bee Gees, Chic's "Le Freak," "Ring My Bell" by one-hitter Anita Ward, and something called "I Love the Nightlife (Disco 'Round)" by the pride of Lawndale, North Carolina, Alicia Bridges.

For a solid three minutes, starting with the opening note, Bridges's lone hit positively smoked in a way that only the best 70s disco could. "I Love the Nightlife" never overpowered, it simply cooked with a steady dance beat that made it impossible to sit still. Plus, the record featured an appealing jazzy swing, owing mostly to Alicia Bridges's unusual lead vocals, which somehow managed to come across as both lazy and powerful. Of course, the best part of the entire tune was undoubtedly the distinctive manner in which Bridges sang the word "action," drawing it out as a deliciously lascivious "ack-shaaawn!"

Between 1978 and 1984, Bridges released three albums of original material: *Alicia Bridges, Play It as It Lays,* and *Hocus Pocus,* with "I Love the Nightlife" taken off the first. None of these LPs remains in print. The disco diva also put out two retrospective compact discs, *I Love the Nightlife* and *Collection,* issued in 1999 and 2002, respectively.

Twenty-five years after setting the Top 40 charts on fire, "I Love the Nightlife (Disco 'Round)" continues to resonate throughout pop culture. Fans of *The Adventures of Priscilla, Queen of the Desert,* a quirky Australian film from 1994 starring Terence Stamp, will fondly recall "I Love the Nightlife's" inclusion on that movie's soundtrack. The song was featured in 1988's *The Last Days of Disco,* as well. Devotees of *The Simpsons* might remember hearing snippets of Alicia Bridges's hit in the "Homer's Phobia," "I'm with Cupid," and "A Milhouse Divided" episodes.

Today, Alicia Bridges has become, in many ways, the musical equivalent of Thomas Pynchon, the enigmatic novelist—no one seems to know exactly where she lives and pictures of the singer are virtually nonexistent.

By the way, artists like Donna Summer ("Bad Girls," "On the Radio," "Dim All the Lights," etc.), Gloria Gaynor ("Never Can Say Goodbye" and "I Will Survive"), and Thelma Houston ("Don't Leave Me This Way") were among the cream of the disco crop, and they all happened to be black. Alicia Bridges, however, to the surprise of most listeners, was white, although her sound was decidedly soulful.

#57

"Our House" by Madness, 1983

Our house, it has a crowd
There's always something happening and it's usually
quite loud

Peaked nationally at #7
Lead singer: Graham McPherson
Written by Chris Foreman and Carl Smyth

"I'll light the fire, you put the flowers in the vase that you bought today." That was the opening line to "Our House." Oh, wait a minute, wrong house! Two different songs called "Our House" have charted in the Top 40: the Crosby, Stills, Nash & Young tune, which was culled from their legendary *Déjà Vu* album from 1970 and peaked at #30, and Madness's "Our House," a track that charged into the Top 10 in the summer of '83.

Madness, who came together in London in 1978 and enjoyed a productive eight-year run, is the perfect example of an outfit achieving household name status in their native country, yet being recalled in America as relatively obscure one-hit wonders. Just consider the many singles that were smashes over in England, but never even came close to denting the U.S. charts: "The Prince," "One Step Beyond," "My Girl," "Night Boat to Cairo," "Cardiac Arrest," "One Better Day," and "House of Fun."

"Our House," like The Mighty Mighty Bosstones' "The Impression That I Get," was that rare pop record incorporating elements of ska, chiefly in the form of energetic brass flourishes throughout. With a cheerful, manic zest, the track explored the daily life of a typical British middle class family—children leaving for school, Mom ironing Dad's shirt, a teenager getting ready for a date, all the ordinary, day-to-day stuff.

In addition to the brassy ska flavor, the thing that really made "Our House" so appealing was Graham McPherson's work on lead vocals. Mind you, McPherson was not possessed of a great voice, but his style fit the material perfectly, as it was drenched in Englishness. Just listening to his pronunciation of phrases and words like "house proud," "always," "small," and "lots" instantly transported one from Pensacola to Piccadilly. Ironically, though, it was this very Britishness that prevented Madness from gaining a solid footing on the FM dial. Take a single like "House of Fun" as an example. In the spring of 1982, it went all the way to #1 in the U.K. and even appeared on *Madness,* the same album that spawned "Our House," yet on this side of the Atlantic, the song never caught sight of the Top 40, and only the most

---

The "Our House" video was an MTV staple in 1983, and rightfully so because it truly captured the New Wave spirit. Incidentally, during the decade of the 80s, no artist spent more weeks on the British pop charts than Madness.

ardent New Waver would be familiar with "House of Fun." Indeed, the tune was so over-the-top Blighty in terms of lyrics and delivery as to be virtually impenetrable to the typical Yankee ear.

In 1985, Madness issued *Mad Not Mad,* which proved to be their last album of original material; a year later they disbanded. Interestingly, though, in 1988, a group called The Madness surfaced, releasing an eponymous CD. This new outfit was composed of Graham McPherson, Chris Foreman, Lee Thompson, Steve Nieve, and Carl Smyth, all of whom had been members of Madness.

#56

"I've Been Thinking About You" by Londonbeat, 1991

Oh, baby, what can I do?
I've been thinking about you

Peaked nationally at #1
Lead singer: Jimmy Chambers
Written by Jimmy Chambers, George Chandler,
    Jimmy Helms, and Will Henshall

Londonbeat was composed of Jimmy Chambers, George Chandler, Jimmy Helms, and Will Henshall, who went by the moniker Willy M. Although the outfit came together in England's capital city, Chandler and Helms hailed from Georgia and Florida, respectively. Chambers, for his part, was Trinidadian, while Willy M was a native Londoner.

"I've Been Thinking About You" was the hit track off an album called *In the Blood.* The single soared to #1 in 1991, spending a total of 14 weeks in the Top 40. Interestingly, at the same time Londonbeat's single was topping the charts, EMF, another British one-hitter, enjoyed their own smash with "Unbelievable." Both "I've Been Thinking About You" and "Unbelievable" proved that great dance music didn't completely vanish with the passing of disco in the early 80s.

Londonbeat's hit record was simultaneously smooth and urgently energetic, an appealing blend of Billy Ocean's "Caribbean Queen" and "Billie Jean" by Michael Jackson, with a splash of Sade's "Sweetest Taboo" for good measure. "I've Been Thinking About You" featured a sound that borrowed from various genres—dance, techno, jazz, soul, R&B, and rock. This mix of musical styles proved enormously effective.

Although seldom heard on radio these days, "I've Been Thinking About You" is no stranger to compilation compact discs, including *36 Hits: 1990–1994, Disco Fox, Vol. 4,* and *Sounds of the 90s.* The song also appears on *Best Remixes, Best! The Singles,* and *Very Best of Londonbeat,* three "best of" CDs issued by Londonbeat.

If you listen to Londonbeat's entire catalogue, it's apparent that the group really suffered from a lack of good material with which to work. The outfit possessed first-class vocal abilities and slick production values, but their songwriting abilities didn't keep pace. Apart from "I've Been Thinking About You," the necessary pop hooks were nowhere to be found on their other offerings.

All told, from 1991 to 1993, Londonbeat released three albums of

In addition to Londonbeat, Julie London and Laurie London are also one-hit wonders. The former scored a #9 record with "Cry Me a River" back in 1955, while the latter enjoyed a #1 smash with "He's Got the Whole World (In His Hands)" in 1958.

By the way, on the heels of "I've Been Thinking About You," Londonbeat charted at #18 in the summer of '91 with "A Better Love." This song, however, did not even rate in the Top 30 in terms of radio airplay, which is why Londonbeat has always been quite correctly viewed as a one-hit wonder.

original tunes: *In the Blood, Harmony,* and *Speak,* only the first of which remains in print.

Today, Londonbeat is a one-hit, 90s memory, though a band called New Londonbeat has surfaced, fronted by Jimmy Helms. As for Will Henshall, he's founded a company called Rocket Network that allows musicians to transfer audio files among their PCs. Jimmy Chambers, who sang lead on "I've Been Thinking About You," and George Chandler continue to be active in the music biz, primarily as background vocalists for U.K.-based acts. Indeed, over the years, Chambers and Chandler have lent their talented voices to artists such as Wham!, Alison Moyet, Paul Young, Deacon Blue, and Swing Out Sister.

#55

"Keep on Dancing" by The Gentrys, 1965

Keep on a' dancin' and a' prancin'
Keep on a' dancin' and a' prancin'

Peaked nationally at #4
Lead singer: Larry Raspberry
Written by Allen Jones and Willie David Young

In 1975, the Bay City Rollers released an album called *Once Upon a Star,* included on which was "Keep on Dancing." The single did not chart. Twenty-two years earlier, a group called The Avantis had waxed the original version of that tune—it didn't chart, either. However, in 1965, The Gentrys, an outfit out of Memphis, Tennessee, got "Keep on Dancing" just right, driving the record all the way to #4.

"Keep on Dancing" began with an energetic drum roll and kept up the enthusiasm for a head-bopping, hip-shaking two minutes and eight seconds. Like "California Sun" by The Rivieras, another classic mid-60s one-hitter, this track was straight ahead, no-frills American rock 'n' roll, doing its best to turn back the musical onslaught known as the British Invasion. The Gentrys imbued their hit with a spontaneous garage sensibility, which has traveled well over the years. Indeed, "Keep on Dancing" sounds as fresh today as it did back when *My Mother, the Car* was airing Tuesday nights on NBC television.

The Gentrys were composed of Bruce Bowles, Bobby Fisher, Jimmy Hart, Jimmy Johnson, Pat Neal, Larry Raspberry, and Larry Wall. It's Raspberry's clear voice that's heard singing lead on "Keep on Dancing." Fans of obscure 80s flicks might recall Larry Raspberry from his acting turn in *This Is Elvis,* where he played the part of Dewey Phillips, the legendary Memphis disk jockey. He also starred in the low-budget horror movie *I Was a Zombie for the F.B.I.* By the way, founding band member Jimmy Hart later achieved fame in the

---

The year 1965 was the height of the British Invasion, with acts like Petula Clark, Herman's Hermits, Freddie & the Dreamers, The Dave Clark Five, and Wayne Fontana & the Mindbenders, not to mention heavyweights such as The Beatles and Stones, dominating the U.S. charts. In addition, '65 saw an abundance of one-hit wonders, both American and English, ride the Top 40. For example, there were The Ad Libs, who reached #8 with "The Boy from New York City." And, of course, the easy-on-the-ears instrumentals "Cast Your Fate to the Wind" by Sounds Orchestral and Horst Jankowski's "A Walk in the Black Forest," which peaked at #10 and #12, respectively. Other memorable one-hitters from the Class of 1965 included Jonathan King's dreamy "Everyone's Gone to the Moon," "The Birds and the Bees" by Jewel Akens, as well as the quintessential feel-bad, doom and gloom song by Oklahoman Barry McGuire, "Eve of Destruction."

world of professional wrestling as Jimmy "The Mouth of the South" Hart, the colorful manager of Hulk Hogan and Honky Tonk Man, among others.

"Keep on Dancing" appeared on a 1965 album of the same name. The LP, no longer in print, also featured "Hang on Sloopy," which another group, The McCoys, rode to #1. In 1999, the Collectables label issued *Cinnamon Girl: The Very Best of The Gentrys*; curiously, this compact disc did not include "Keep on Dancing." How can a "best of" compilation from a one-hit wonder *not* contain that act's lone hit? "Keep on Dancing," though, can be found on numerous CD collections, including: *Frat Rock! 54 of the All-Time Greatest Rock 'n' Roll Tunes, Classic Rock: 1965–The Beat Goes On, Wild Thing: 60s Rock Bands,* as well as *Rock 'n' Roll Dance Party.*

#54

"The Curly Shuffle" by Jump 'n the Saddle Band, 1984

We don't like to fight and we don't like to scuffle
But we dance all night doing the Curly Shuffle

Peaked nationally at #15
Lead singer: Peter Quinn
Written by Peter Quinn

During the 60s and early 70s, pop music's heyday on the AM dial, program directors at Top 40 giants like WABC, WFIL, KFRC, and KHJ were not afraid of an eclectic playlist. Play "The Candy Man" by Sammy Davis, Jr., followed by Neil Young's "Heart of Gold"? Sure, why not! Mix a little "Somethin' Stupid" by Frank and Nancy Sinatra in with The Stones' "Ruby Tuesday"? Right on! What's more, there was even room for novelty numbers like Chuck Berry's "My Ding-a-Ling," "Kung Fu Fighting" by Carl Douglas, and The New Vaudeville Band's "Winchester Cathedral."

Well, fast forward to the year 1984 and radio programmers have tightened up their formats noticeably, so it's surprising when a silly ditty called "The Curly Shuffle" starts climbing the charts, peaking at a very respectable #15.

"The Curly Shuffle" was an enthusiastic, heartfelt tribute to Larry Fine, Moe Howard, and of course, his brother, Curly Howard, a trio known the world over as The Three Stooges. Yes, the song was undoubtedly goofy, replete with "nyuk, nyuks" and crazy sound effects, but make no mistake, this tune swung and rocked harder than any "Karma Chameleon" or "Caribbean Queen" ever could. So, when folks dismissively lumped "The Curly Shuffle" together with genuinely lightweight novelty one-hitters like, say, "Disco Duck" by Rick Dees or "Pac-Man Fever" by Buckner & Garcia, they just weren't paying close attention. This record was polished Texas swing in the best tradition of Commander Cody & His Lost Planet Airmen and Asleep at the Wheel, nicely blended with a bluesy dollop of Southside Johnny & the Asbury Jukes.

On Monday, July 18, 1983, Jump 'n the Saddle Band went into the Acme Recording Studio at 3821 N. Southport Avenue, less than a mile from Chicago's Wrigley Field, to wax what was to become their lone chart success, "The Curly Shuffle." The outfit's personnel on that midsummer's day was Peter Quinn, lead vocals; T.C. Furlong, steel gui-

---

"Pass the Dutchie" by Musical Youth; Bobby McFerrin's "Don't Worry Be Happy;" "Puttin' on the Ritz" by Taco; "Mickey" by Toni Basil; Carl Douglas's "Kung Fu Fighting;" Randy Newman's "Short People;" "Funkytown" by Lipps, Inc.; "Pop Muzik" by M; and Bob & Doug McKenzie's "Take Off" were all memorable one-hitters that, in the spirit of "The Curly Shuffle," approached the listener with a good-natured wink and a mischievous smile.

tar; Anne Schwartz, bass guitar and backing vocals; Barney Schwartz, electric guitar and backing vocals; Vincent Dee, drums; and Tom Trinka, saxophone.

Following the brief recording session, a 45 r.p.m. version of "The Curly Shuffle" was pressed on the Acme label, quickly finding its way onto the Chicagoland airwaves. The song became a local smash, which brought it to the attention of Atlantic Records. By early 1984, Casey Kasem was telling listeners around the world, "Moving up three notches to #15 this week is a group from The Windy City. . . ." Jump 'n the Saddle Band was off to a galloping start.

However, producing that always-elusive, and vitally important second hit proved impossible, and Jump 'n the Saddle Band faded faster than the Cubs in a September pennant race. Yes, a follow-up single, "It Should Have Been Me," was issued, but it tanked. Game over.

Today, two original Jump 'n the Saddle Band members, Peter Quinn and Tom Trinka, gig with a group called Skip Towne & the Greyhounds, playing bar-band blues and old time rock 'n' roll.

#53

"In the House of Stone and Light" by Martin Page, 1995

Holy Lady, show me my soul
Tell me of that place where I must surely go

Peaked nationally at #14
Lead singer: Martin Page
Written by Martin Page

The Beatles were once asked, "What is it that *you* have that the other bands don't?" Without hesitation, George Harrison responded by uttering two simple words: "Press agents."

Ah, the undeniable power and influence of flacks. Would Marc Cohn, for example, be as well known today as, say, Michael Bolton if Atlantic, Cohn's record label, had really put the publicity machine into high gear on his behalf back in the early 90s? By the same token, with respect to the subject at hand, Martin Page, what kept the brass over at Mercury Records from working effectively with this unquestionably talented Englishman to mold him into the next Peter Gabriel?

As a pop songwriter, Page's *curriculum vitae* speaks for itself. A few highlights: He co-penned "We Built This City," which Mickey Thomas, Grace Slick, and the rest of the Starship rode all the way to #1 in 1985; he was co-writer of Go West's "King of Wishful Thinking," a Top 10 single during the summer of 1990; and he co-wrote "These Dreams," Heart's mid-80s smash. Performers as diverse as Kim Carnes, Bryan Ferry, The Commodores, John Waite, and Robbie Roberston have also waxed material written by Martin Page.

In 1994, this world-class tunesmith, a man who could probably dash off a hit song while waiting in the check-out line at Safeway, is-

---

Bob Marley landed three singles on the American charts. Well, actually, that's not true, as Marley never, neither as a solo act nor with his Wailers, scored a Top 40 hit, not even one. The pride of Jamaica is a classic *no*-hit wonder.

"I Shot the Sheriff"? Marley's version didn't chart. "Stir It Up"? While Johnny Nash's cover reached #12 in '73, Bob Marley's stiffed chart-wise. "One Love," "Is This Love," "Redemption Song," "Get Up, Stand Up," and "No Woman, No Cry"—none of these terrific records by Marley dented the Top 40.

Other relatively high-profile no-hit wonders include The Velvet Underground, Phish, The Jesus & Mary Chain, The Smiths, Joan Armatrading, The Pogues, Mahavishnu Orchestra, and The Pousette-Dart Band.

sued his first album, *In the House of Stone and Light,* off which came the title track, spending an impressive 26 weeks in the Top 40.

Page's vocals on "In the House of Stone and Light" were a radio-friendly blend of Rod Stewart, Steve Winwood, and Peter Gabriel— slickly produced, British blue-eyed soul. The overall sound of Martin Page's voice was comfortably mainstream. Surprisingly, though, coming as they did from such an accomplished writer, the song's lyrics were not very memorable. Indeed, for a record that charted for a full six months, receiving massive airplay in the process, few listeners could get a firm handle on just what "In the House of Stone and Light" was all about. Unless you were sitting down with the words right in front of you, the whole message was rather inscrutable in a New Agey kind of way. Page was going all Marin County and Sedona, Arizona, on us, singing about shamans, inner children, and crooked paths. Perhaps, however, these cabalistic references were at the core of the song's chart success and longevity: it's hard to tire of a single whose meaning you're still attempting to figure out.

Today, Martin Page makes his home in the Los Angeles suburb of Encino. Nearly ten years after releasing his debut CD, the native of Southampton, England, is sitting on a completed second album, as he shops for a suitable record deal.

#52

"Signs"
by Five Man Electrical Band, 1971

Sign, sign, everywhere a sign
Blocking out the scenery, breaking my mind

Peaked nationally at #3
Lead singer: Les Emmerson
Written by Les Emmerson

"Beneath its surface, though, a heart's cry for a saner, sweeter, more thoughtful and restrained existence." So wrote Richard Ford in the *Chicago Tribune* about Jay McInerney's novel *Bright Lights, Big City*. He might just as easily have been writing about a classic piece of early 70s AM gold called "Signs."

Five Man Electrical Band hailed from the same place as Paul Anka and Alanis Morissette: Ottawa, Canada's capital city. The group was composed of Les Emmerson, brothers Mike and Rick Belanger, Ted Gerow, and Brian Rading.

"Signs" was taken off of *Good-byes & Butterflies,* a groovily named LP that kind of belied the band's gritty, bar-band pedigree. The song began with an up-tempo, hard-charging drum and organ riff straight out of The Spencer Davis Group's "Gimme' Some Lovin'," which gave way to a buzz saw electric guitar, then, quite unexpectedly, the tune's energy dropped and Les Emmerson's clear, prayerful vocals took over.

At its core, "Signs" was a protest tune in the best tradition of The Buffalo Springfield's "For What It's Worth," "The Times They Are A-Changin'" by Bob Dylan, and Woody Guthrie's "This Land Is Your Land." Unlike those other songs, though, Five Man Electrical Band's

#3 record made its point with a certain engaging, earnest goofiness.

Interestingly, when "Signs" was first released as a 45 on the MGM label, it was actually the B-side to a track called "Hello Melinda, Goodbye." The disk totally stiffed, both sides. Indeed, MGM Records was so disappointed in the commercial performance of the boys from Ottawa that they completely cut them loose in the wake of the "Hello Melinda, Goodbye"/"Signs" flop. The group, however, managed to rebound, hooking up with the Lionel Entertainment Corporation, a division of Lionel Corporation, the famed manufacturer of toy trains.

In early 1971, confident in its newest act's existing store of material, Lionel Entertainment decided to issue a Five Man Electrical Band album on the Lionel label, the aforementioned *Good-byes & Butterflies.* Once again, "Signs" was put out as a single, only this time it caught fire, climbing all the way to the Top 5.

Five Man Electrical Band spent most of '71 and '72 on the road performing, opening for the likes of Jefferson Airplane, The Allman Brothers, and fellow Canadians Bachman-Turner Overdrive. During this period, the group also released *Coming of Age,* the follow-up to *Good-byes & Butterflies.* "Absolutely Right," culled from *Coming of Age,* landed at #26 on the charts, so Five Man Electrical Band was *not* a one-hit wonder, right? Wrong. A 22-year-old right-fielder smacks 41 homers (*i.e.,* scores a #3 smash) in his rookie season. During his sophomore effort, however, he manages only 13 dingers (*i.e.,* a #26 record)—well, you get the point. Throughout the history of pop music, with certain rare exceptions such as The Grateful Dead, long-term success has always been predicated on the ability to consistently produce radio-friendly hit singles, something Les Emmerson & Co. were never able to achieve.

All told, between 1970 and 1973, Five Man Electrical Band produced four full-length LPs; in addition, in 1996, a collection called *Absolutely Right: The Best of Five Man Electrical Band* was issued by Polydor.

#51

"Groove Is in the Heart" by Deee-Lite, 1990

The chills that you spill up my back
Keep me filled with satisfaction

Peaked nationally at #4
Lead singer: Lady Miss Kier
Written by Deee-Lite

It's 403 miles, give or take, from Youngstown, Ohio, to New York, New York. From Tokyo to The Big Apple, it's 6,760 miles. However, New York City is a scant 4,678 miles from the Ukrainian capital of Kiev. Well, in the words of one-hitter Oleta Adams: "I don't care how you get here, just get here if you can."

Deee-Lite was composed of Lady Miss Kier, Towa Tei, and DJ Dmitry, natives of Youngstown, Tokyo, and Kiev, respectively. The Manhattan-based group enjoyed a 10-year run, 1986 through 1996. Yet, in their decade together, the trio visited the Top 40 just once, that being in 1990 when "Groove Is in the Heart" shot to #4.

"Groove Is in the Heart," which spent three months on the charts, was a fantastical amalgamation of Donna Summer disco, George Clinton funk, Pet Shop Boys synth, and Us3 jazz/rap. Indeed, it would be difficult to name another song that so successfully combined as many disparate musical styles. Of course, it would be *impossible* to point to another track that references Dr. Seuss's *Horton Hears a Who,* the boiled corn kernel concoction known as succotash, and Hawaiian hula dancing.

The twilight of George Herbert Walker Bush's tenure in the White House coincided with an interesting era in pop, a period when highly danceable records like "Groove Is in the Heart," "Gonna Make You

Sweat (Everybody Dance Now)" by C+C Music Factory, and London-beat's "I've Been Thinking About You" were saturating the airwaves. Actually, it only stood to reason that during a time of economic malaise and tensions overseas due to the Gulf War, listeners would be drawn to upbeat, shake-your-bones grooves as an effective means of forgetting their worries.

Deee-Lite's lone hit came off an album called *World Clique,* the cover of which alone was worth the price of the compact disc. There, against a backdrop of stars and multi-colored daisies, were the three Gotham City hipsters: Towa Tei sporting white sneakers and a pair of striped pants that resembled nothing so much as a television test pattern; Lady Miss Kier, all bright yellow slacks and four-inch heels; and DJ Dmitry, sharply turned out in his green long-sleeved shirt and two-toned vest. In fact, all of Deee-Lite's album covers were psyche-delic eye candy in the spirit of The Beatles' *Magical Mystery Tour* and *Abraxas* by Santana.

"Vote, Baby, Vote" and "I Had a Dream I Was Falling Through a Hole in the Ozone Layer" were two of the songs featured on Deee-Lite's sophomore CD, *Infinity Within.* And that, essentially, is all you need to know in terms of understanding the group's status today as one-hit wonders. Encouraging citizens to exercise their voting rights, while so-cially commendable, is not, and never will be, the stuff of chart success.

In the years since the outfit's demise in '96, all of the former Deee-Liters have kept low profiles. DJ Dmitry, in 2000, issued a solo effort on the TVT label, *Screams of Consciousness,* an LP that could charita-bly be described as obscure. As for Lady Miss Kier, who, incidentally, is married to DJ Dmitry, she's turned the bulk of her attention to a ca-reer as a graphic designer. Towa Tei, for his part, has released a half-dozen or so avant-garde albums, the most recent being 1999's *Last Century Modern.*

Finally, just in case you ever find yourself as a contestant on VH-1's *Rock 'n' Roll Jeopardy,* Lady Miss Kier was born Kieren Kirby, while DJ Dmitry is actually Dmitry Brill and Towa Tei would be better known to his parents as Doug Wa-Chung.

#50

"Kansas City"
by Wilbert Harrison, 1959

They got some crazy little women there
And I'm gonna get me one

Peaked nationally at #1
Lead singer: Wilbert Harrison
Written by Jerry Leiber and Mike Stoller

Little Willie Littlefield, a largely forgotten bluesman originally from Houston, Texas, issued a single in the early 50s called "K.C. Lovin'." The track featured Littlefield's understated vocals, backed by a bouncing bass line and a bleating sax. It was superb rhythm and blues, occupying the top position on the national R&B chart for nearly two months back in 1952. What's more, you could even consider the tune one of the very first bona fide pieces of rock 'n' roll, pre-dating the likes of "Shake, Rattle and Roll" and "(We're Gonna) Rock Around the Clock" by Bill Haley and His Comets by a good two years. In 1959, the Fury label released "Kansas City" by Wilbert Harrison, a 30-year-old North Carolinian. The record was basically a rejiggering of "K.C. Lovin'." Harrison replaced the bounce found in Little Willie Littlefield's version with an insistent, hypnotizing shuffle, while the saxophone gave way to an electric guitar. And, where the original employed a rather restrained style of singing, Harrison juiced up the lead vocals on "Kansas City." All this tinkering worked well, as the song zoomed to #1, spending three months on the charts.

Over the years, "Kansas City" has been covered by a remarkably wide variety of artists, including The Beatles, Libby Titus, Scatman Crothers, Louis Prima, Little Richard, and Muddy Waters. Even Brenda "Rockin' Around the Christmas Tree" Lee, on her *Wiedersehn Ist*

Wunderschon album, jumped on the musical bandwagon, recording "Kansas City" in German. Interestingly, though, besides Wilbert Harrison, only Trini Lopez, of "If I Had a Hammer" and "Lemon Tree" fame, ever managed to crack the Top 40 with "Kansas City," reaching a modest #23 in 1964.

Eleven years after scoring a #1 smash, Harrison waxed a tune entitled "Let's Work Together" that peaked at #32. For those who would then argue that the man is, in fact, a *two*-hit wonder, well, a group called the Spin Doctors bears mentioning. Remember this outfit from New York City? They landed at #17 in 1992 with "Little Miss Can't Be Wrong," followed up by "Two Princes" at #7. One Top 20 record plus a Top 10—now, *that* adds up to a legitimate two-hitter. On the other hand, Wilbert Harrison's tepid #32 a full *decade* after having the Top Dog—that equals a one-hit wonder. Incidentally, "Let's Work Together," which Harrison wrote, was later covered by Canned Heat, George Thorogood, Climax Blues Band, as well as the Kentucky Headhunters.

Wilbert Harrison passed away in his native North Carolina during the fall of 1994 at the age of 65. However, since his death, interest in his music continues, as evidenced by the 2000 issuance of *Kansas City: The Best of Wilbert Harrison* on the Aim label.

"Kansas City" was written by Jerry Leiber and Mike Stoller, who indisputably rank among the best songwriting teams in pop history. Remember "On Broadway" by The Drifters? Leiber and Stoller wrote it. How about the 50s classic "Hound Dog"? Again, penned by Leiber and Stoller. "Stand by Me," which Ben E. King rode to #4 in 1961? Yep, you guessed it, Leiber and Stoller. "Charlie Brown," "Riot in Cell Block #9," "Poison Ivy," "Yakety Yak," and "Searchin'"— each of these famous tunes sprang from the fertile musical imaginations of Jerry Leiber and Mike Stoller.

#49

"The Promise" by When in Rome, 1988

When you need a friend, don't look to a stranger
You know in the end, I'll always be there

Peaked nationally at #11
Lead singer: Clive Farrington
Written by Clive Farrington, Andrew Mann, and
  Michael Floreale

With a pulsating, mesmerizing techno beat, "The Promise" stands as one of the best dance tracks ever waxed. Fifteen years after its release, When in Rome's lone chart hit still sounds fresh, capable of moving a million feet. From a one-hit wonder perspective, "The Promise" gets grouped in the "Mary's Prayer" and "Breakout" family: sophisticated, late 80s British pop. Sadly, though, groups such as Danny Wilson (yes, Danny Wilson was the name of a *band,* not a person), Swing Out Sister, and When in Rome would never even catch a sniff of today's Top 40. Consider the following eye-opening sentence taken from a June 2002 Associated Press dispatch from London: "Last month, for the first time since 1963, there were no British artists in the Billboard Hot 100 singles chart—and now some in the industry here [in Britain] are calling for a music 'embassy' to promote their artists in the United States." No room on the American charts for the land that gave us everyone from The Beatles to Petula Clark to Led Zeppelin to Phil Collins to Oasis? Astonishing!

The band issued just one album, 1988's *When in Rome,* featuring "The Promise" as the lead cut. The song has also appeared on compilation CDs like *A Trip Back to the 80s,* the crazily named *Can't Get This No More!,* and *Living in Oblivion: The 80's Greatest Hits, Vol. 5.* By the way, these "Romans" from Manchester, England, tried to follow up the success of their #11 single with a tune called "Heaven Knows." This record, heavy on synthesizer, light on a memorable hook, peaked at a disappointing #95.

Andrew Mann, Clive Farrington, and Michael Floreale were the members of When in Rome. Interestingly, the trio had previously performed with an obscure outfit called Leisure, about which virtually nothing is known except that it included a pretty singer by the name of Corrine Drewery, who later joined forces with Andy Connell and Martin Jackson to form the aforementioned Swing Out Sister.

In listening to When in Rome's lone compact disc in its entirety, it's obvious why the band could manage to dent the Top 40 only once: Apart from "The Promise," the other nine tracks are go-nowhere aural wallpaper. It's really a bit of a head-scratcher, though. How an obviously talented group could start off with such a memorable, well-crafted song and then completely fizzle is genuinely puzzling.

The Top 40 format on AM radio was running on fumes by the time the 80s rolled around. By decade's end, all the legendary music stations from the 60s and 70s, AM powerhouses such as WABC, WNBC, WRKO, WLS, and KHJ, had stopped playing pop/rock and adopted new formats, mostly talk-based. What follows, though, is the memorable disk jockey line-up of Chicago's legendary Top 40 outlet WLS from the year 1980:

5:30 A.M. to 10:00 A.M.	— Larry Lujack
10:00 A.M. to 2:00 P.M.	— Tommy Edwards
2:00 P.M. to 6:00 P.M.	— Bob Sirott
6:00 P.M. to 10:00 P.M.	— John Records Landecker
10:00 P.M. to 2:00 A.M.	— Jeff Davis
2:00 A.M. to 5:30 A.M.	— Yvonne Daniels

#48

"Sunny Came Home" by Shawn Colvin, 1997

Sunny came home with a list of names
She didn't believe in transcendence

Peaked nationally at #7
Lead singer: Shawn Colvin
Written by Shawn Colvin and John Leventhal

Remember "Luka" from 1987, Suzanne Vega's heartbreaking single concerning child abuse? If you listen closely, you can hear Shawn Colvin singing softly in the background. Well, ten years later, Colvin was very much in the foreground with "Sunny Came Home," her own Top 10 smash that earned Song of the Year and Record of the Year honors.

"Sunny Came Home" kicked off an album called *A Few Small Repairs*. The song, which featured a distinct folky, country flavor, told the story of a woman at the end of her rope, Sunny, who desired to light the entire world ablaze and then step right into the flames, putting an end to some unspecified pain. As pop records go, it was definitely on the bleak, desperate side. Inasmuch as "Sunny Came Home" shared space with "Suicide Alley," "Trouble," and "Get Out of This House," it's fair to say that the music press was not hailing *A Few Small Repairs* as the feel-good CD of 1997.

Shawn Colvin's lone hit meshed perfectly with the mid- to late-90s musical *zeitgeist,* that being the era of radio's fascination with female solo acts delivering deliberately paced, searching fare. Witness "Every Day Is a Winding Road" and "A Change Would Do You Good" by Sheryl Crow, as well as Sarah McLachlan's "Adia" and "Building a Mystery," not to mention Paula Cole and her "I Don't Want to Wait."

Shawn Colvin was born in 1956, as were fellow one-hitters Debby Boone, Amii Stewart, Chris Isaak, Peter Schilling, and Rex Smith. Pat Boone's daughter, Debby, blitzed the Top 40 with "You Light Up My Life," a record that spent an astounding 10 weeks in the #1 position in the fall of 1977. Of course, Amii Stewart enjoyed her own #1 song, "Knock on Wood," which charted in 1979, the same year Rex Smith peaked at #10 with "You Take My Breath Away."

As for Messrs. Isaak and Schilling, the former had a #6 tune in 1991, "Wicked Game," and the latter reached #14 with 1983's "Major Tom (Coming Home)."

Not surprisingly, Colvin, Crow, and Cole all took part in the famous Lilith Fair, the women-performers-only concert series organized by McLachlan.

Born in South Dakota as Shanna Colvin, the singer landed in Manhattan in her mid-20s, cutting her teeth as a folkie at legendary Bleecker Street clubs such as Kenny's Castaways and The Bitter End. She also hooked up with New York City's musical theater community, performing alongside Maria "Midnight at the Oasis" Muldaur in a Broadway production of *Pump Boys and Dinettes.* Colvin even did a turn with the Red Clay Ramblers, the bluegrass ensemble from North Carolina that provided the musical accompaniment to Sam Shepard's acclaimed play *A Lie of the Mind,* the original staging of which starred Harvey Keitel and Amanda Plummer.

When Shawn Colvin—now approaching age 50—finally broke through to a wide audience on the strength of her 1997 Grammy haul for "Sunny Came Home," few mainstream listeners realized that seven years earlier she had already snagged a Grammy for Best Contemporary Folk Recording for a compact disc entitled *Steady On.*

Today, Colvin has nine albums to her credit, six of which remain in print. She also tours constantly, playing clubs like The Fillmore in

San Francisco, Las Vegas's House of Blues, and The Casino Ballroom in New Hampshire.

#47

"Rock On" by David Essex, 1974

See her shake on the movie screen
Jimmy Dean . . . James Dean

Peaked nationally at #5
Lead singer: David Essex
Written by David Essex

Starting in the early 70s and continuing on through today, no fewer than 28 full-length David Essex LPs have been issued, meaning one could start spinning his albums at breakfast and still be playing his music well after the dinner dishes had been cleared. That being said, on streets from Mobile to Minneapolis, Essex would be virtually unknown but for three minutes and twenty-four seconds of wax pressed some 30 years ago.

In 1974, a year when AM radio giants like WABC, KFRC, and KHJ were dispensing groovy vibes from coast to coast in the form of Blue Swede's "Hooked on a Feeling," "Rock the Boat" by The Hues Corporation, and John Denver's "Sunshine on My Shoulders," "Rock On" was a welcome breath of cool, dark air.

The track begins with a deep, atmospheric bass line, which rumbles steadily throughout the tune. Then Essex's vocal, full of reverb, kicks in, echoing and bouncing from one line to the next. The overall effect is rather sinister, and surprisingly so for a simple record that is essentially about how much rock 'n' roll is, and has been since the 1950s, such a big part of teenage life.

"Rock On," from an album of the same name, proved to be David

Essex's lone charter in the United States; however, he can boast in excess of two dozen hit singles in his native U.K. It's fascinating, and not a little bit perplexing, that an artist could enjoy so much success in Britain, while at the same time being the quintessential one-hit wonder across the pond. Maybe it comes down to what the playwright George Bernard Shaw said, "England and America are two countries divided by a common language." It's also conceivable that because Essex always fancied himself an actor as much as a singer, his recording career was never taken seriously in America. A partial examination of his acting resume reveals the kind of work that would scarcely register on the radar screens of Top 40 fans in, say, Chicago or Miami: a West End staging of *Godspell,* role of Jesus; played Che in the original London production of *Evita*; did a turn as Don Pedro, an evil Spaniard, in a Japanese movie called *Shogun Warrior*; and portrayed Nick Freeman in *Silver Dream Racer*, a 1980 flick that included Beau Bridges and Cristina "Flamingo Road" Raines.

David Essex did his best acting work, though, in a pair of truly obscure British films: *That'll Be the Day* and its sequel, *Stardust*, from 1973 and 1974, respectively. In both these pictures, he played the part of Jim Maclaine, an English rocker somewhat patterned on John Lennon. By the way, director Michael Apted, who was to gain Hollywood acclaim through his work on *Coal Miner's Daughter* and *Gorky Park*, directed *Stardust*.

Today, Essex, or should I say *David Essex, O.B.E.*, as he was awarded the prestigious Order of the British Empire by Queen Elizabeth in 1999, remains an extremely popular entertainer in England, appear-

---

In 1972, T. Rex, the glam rockers from England, released an album entitled *The Slider* that featured a Marc Bolan–written song called "Rock On." This song did not dent the charts. In fact, like David Essex, T. Rex managed to score only one hit record in the United States, the #10 "Bang a Gong (Get It On)" from the spring of '72.

ing regularly on television, cutting new CDs, and playing concert halls from Brighton to Blackpool.

#46

"Tired of Toein' the Line" by Rocky Burnette, 1980

If you want to get rid of me
Baby, baby, baby, you're doing fine

Peaked nationally at #8
Lead singer: Rocky Burnette
Written by Rocky Burnette and Ron Coleman

In 1980, when Billy Joel clearly saw the so-called New Wave rolling in, he kind of shrugged and sang: "Next phase, New Wave, dance craze, anyways, it's still rock 'n' roll to me." As for Rocky Burnette, well, he followed Joel's lead by releasing an album called *The Son of Rock and Roll*. Sensing a decade that was destined to be dominated by Thompson Twins and Pet Shop Boys, the Joels and Burnettes of the music world seemed to be saying, "Hey, we can hear the synthesizers on the horizon, so screw it—let's break out the Stratocasters and just rock one last time!"

"Tired of Toein' the Line," the lone hit from *The Son of Rock and Roll*, was get-your-skinny-New-Wave-ass-off-the-stage American rock and *freakin'* roll. All punchy lead guitar and clear, strong vocals, this was the sort of record that demanded to be played at full volume. In fact, 1980 was a year that spawned two Top 10 singles that sounded particularly good when they were cranked all the way to eleven: "Ride Like the Wind" by Christopher Cross and Rocky Burnette's "Tired of Toein' the Line."

During the summer of '80, at the height of Burnette's chart run, there was no avoiding his #8 smash: on both radio *and* television, the song dominated the airwaves from Maine to Malibu. In a span of mere weeks, "Tired of Toein' the Line" was featured on *American Bandstand, Don Kirshner's Rock Concert, The Midnight Special,* and *Solid Gold*. Top 40–wise, however, that period, coinciding with Jimmy Carter winding down his stay at 1600 Pennsylvania Avenue, proved to be Burnette's first and last hurrah. But, quite frankly, if ever an artist could convincingly plead extenuating circumstances as the reason for his status as a one-hit wonder, it would have to be Rocky Burnette. Just as "Tired of Toein' the Line" was paving the way for a follow-up single, not to mention album, EMI America, Burnette's label, went belly-up. Ouch! The gears on the promotion machine, so vital to the commercial success of any pop/rock act, came to a grinding halt. Ironically, EMI's overseas operations, which were independent of EMI America, continued flacking the Memphis native's music, making Burnette more popular in Australia than Arizona.

No discussion of Rocky Burnette is complete without nods to Johnny Burnette, his dad, and Dorsey Burnette, his uncle. Johnny, who died at the age of 30 in a boating accident on Northern California's Clear Lake, landed four tunes in the Top 40, including "You're Sixteen," which, coincidentally, peaked at the #8 position, just like his son's "Tired of Toein' the Line." By the way, a father-child Top 10 connection is rather rare—aside from Johnny Burnette and Rocky Burnette, it's a short list: Rufus Thomas and Carla Thomas; Pat Boone and Debby Boone; Frank Sinatra and Nancy Sinatra; John Lennon and Julian Lennon; and Nat "King" Cole and Natalie Cole. As for Dorsey, Johnny's older brother, he scored with "(There Was A) Tall Oak Tree," a #23 song from 1960.

Today, looking at age 50, Burnette has four albums to his credit, including 2002's *Hip Shakin' Baby: A Tribute to Johnny and Dorsey Burnette*. And, even though *The Son of Rock and Roll* LP never made the transition from wax to compact disc, "Tired of Toein' the Line" is still available on *Radio Daze: Pop Hits of the '80s, Vol. 3*, where it finds itself in the good one-hit wonder company of "Who'll Be the

Fool Tonight" by Larsen-Feiten Band and Ali Thomson's "Take a Little Rhythm."

#45

"Mouth" by Merril Bainbridge, 1996

When I kiss your mouth, I want to taste it

Peaked nationally at #4
Lead singer: Merril Bainbridge
Written by Merril Bainbridge

When asked if she knew all along that "Mouth" was going to be such a huge success, Merril Bainbridge said with refreshing candor, "It's such a gamble, you have no idea what's going to be a hit."

Bainbridge and her "Mouth" spent an amazing six months in the Top 40. What's even more remarkable, though, was the Australian singer's precipitous fall from the pop charts: a #4 smash on the charts for 25 weeks, then oblivion.

"Mouth" was a flirty, randy single wrapped in a bright, innocent package. Bainbridge sang about erotic kissing, slapping, and getting turned on, but she did so with a light, jaunty touch that disguised the tune's underlying sexuality. Can you imagine, say, a shy high school junior being subtly and quite unexpectedly seduced by his 28-year-old trigonometry teacher during a private, after-hours help session? Well, this was kind of the vibe that emanated from "Mouth." Incidentally, the two most suggestive one-hit wonders on our survey, Bainbridge's record and "I Touch Myself" by the Divinyls, were both products of the Land Down Under.

To date, Merril Bainbridge has released just two albums: *The Garden* and *Between the Days*, her Top 5 charter appearing on the former, which, surprisingly, is no longer in print. However, "Mouth" is still available on any number of compilation CDs, including *Dance Across the Universe, Vol. 1, Australia 2000,* and *Soft Pop.*

After listening to several of Bainbridge's songs, it's obvious why she's a one-hitter: her voice is certainly pleasant and distinctive on every track, the musicianship is superb, but only "Mouth" possesses the kind of memorable, infectious pop hook that's required to make a hit single, which points to the importance of strong songwriting. And Bainbridge, who has had a hand in the penning of all her tunes, just hasn't been able to come up with a bounty of commercially effective material. By the way, Rochelle, a female singer who is originally from Bermuda, of all places, waxed a cover of "Mouth" that was heard on the Showtime series *Queer as Folk.* Rochelle's version was also part of *Loud & Proud: Ultimate Gay Anthems.* Evidently, "Mouth," or at least the rendition by this Bermudian, has become a favorite within the gay community.

Over the past few years, the pretty blonde who was raised in the northern suburbs of Melbourne has kept a low musical profile, though, on occasion, she's flexed her creative muscles. For example, in 1999, she issued a single called "Sydney from a 747," which was featured in an Aussie film short, *Sydney: Story of a City.* Then, a year later, the Bainbridge-penned "You're the Only One" found its way onto John Farnham's compact disc entitled *33 1/3.* In addition, as of early 2003, her current label, Gotham Records, reported that a third

> Merril Bainbridge wasn't the only artist during the 90s to release a tune called "Mouth." Back in '96, Bush, the British grungers, put out a CD, *Razorblade Suitcase,* the seventh cut of which was "Mouth." This track was written by Gavin Rossdale, Bush's lead singer. And, two years prior to that, in 1994, an eccentrically named outfit from Manhattan called Melting Hopefuls, which specialized in folky pop, showcased their own "Mouth" on the *Space Flyer* album.

Merril Bainbridge album was in the works, and that fans of the singer could "expect something very fresh and innovative this time around."

#44

"Sukiyaki" by Kyu Sakamoto, 1963

Ue o muite aruko / *I look up when I walk*
Namida ga kobore naiyouni / *So the tears won't fall*

Peaked nationally at #1
Lead singer: Kyu Sakamoto
Written by Rokusuke Ei

Imagine a pop song—a one-hit wonder at that!—inspiring a postage stamp. Can you picture, for example, Musical Youth's "Pass the Dutchie" on a stamp? Or, how about "Cruel to Be Kind" by Nick Lowe? Well, in the late 90s, the Japanese Postal Service issued a 50-yen postage stamp that featured a whimsical drawing of a young man walking on green grass, looking skyward at the clouds and stars. This stamp honored one of Japan's most beloved tunes, a record from the early 60s called "Ue O Muite Aruko," which translates, more or less, to "I Look Up When I Walk."

"Ue O Muite Aruko" was a #1 smash during John F. Kennedy's last summer as president. But transistor-toting teens in, say, San Francisco, unlike their counterparts across the Pacific in Sapporo, would have been completely baffled by that title, because they knew the single simply as "Sukiyaki." Of course, it speaks volumes about the cultural *zeitgeist* of 1963 that the brass over at 1750 N. Vine, Capitol Records' Hollywood headquarters, decided to go with such a goofy, stereotypical name, as opposed to the perfectly fine translation of "I Look Up When I Walk," but that's another story.

The late Kyu Sakamoto sang every word of "Sukiyaki" in Japanese, something unique in American chart history. In fact, only two acts from The Land of the Rising Sun have *ever* dented the Top 40: Sakamoto and an outfit from Tokyo called Pink Lady, who, singing in English, limped to #37 with the now-totally-forgotten "Kiss in the Dark" in 1979. Kyu Sakamoto and Pink Lady—both from Japan, both one-hitters.

Even though listeners in the States hadn't the foggiest idea what Sakamoto was crooning about, his voice was so expressive that it transcended any linguistic barriers. Naturally, a large measure of credit for "Sukiyaki's" success must also be given to Rokusuke Ei, the man who wrote such moving lyrics for Kyu Sakamoto to interpret. And if ever words came from a place of pure emotional despair, they were Ei's, as he scribbled his tune in the aftermath of a heartbreaking split with Meiko Nakamura, a star of Japanese cinema back in the 60s and 70s. What flowed from the songwriter's pen was perhaps the saddest, most achingly beautiful lover's lament in pop history, a tale of a fellow walking alone, his head tilted up so the world wouldn't see his tears falling.

Today, Rokusuke Ei is famous throughout Japan as one of the country's best-selling novelists. Sadly, though, Kyu Sakamoto died in a plane crash in 1985, leaving behind a wife and two children.

Forty years after its release, Oldies stations still include "Sukiyaki" in their rotations, with most DJs and program directors still blissfully unaware that the tune has absolutely nothing to do with a dish you might order at the local Benihana. By the way, Taste of Honey, the band out of Southern California that introduced a disco-obsessed nation to the phrase "boogie oogie ooggie" in the summer of 1978, waxed an English language cover of "Sukiyaki" that peaked at #3 in 1981. This version did, however, feature one word in Japanese, *"say-onara"*—in fact, it's seductively whispered at the very end of the track as the record fades out. In the mid 90s, a one-hit wonder outfit from Baltimore called 4 P.M. gave Taste of Honey's "Sukiyaki" the street-corner a cappella treatment, earning themselves a #8 single in the process.

#43

"One Night in Bangkok" by Murray Head, 1985

Get Thai'd! You're talking to a tourist
Whose every move's among the purist

Peaked nationally at #3
Lead singer: Murray Head
Written by Benny Andersson, Bjorn Ulvaeus, and Tim Rice

The late Jerry Garcia of Grateful Dead fame once quipped: "Our audience is like people who like licorice. Not everybody likes licorice, but the people who like licorice *really* like licorice." Well, the same could be said for "One Night in Bangkok"—it's one of those songs that folks either seem to love or hate, no in-between.

The overwhelming majority of pop songs concern themselves with themes of love: new love, lost love, unrequited love, you get the idea. So, how refreshing it was, not to mention completely out of left field, when DJs started spinning a record about high-level international chess. A Top 5 smash about the mysterious, esoteric world of Bobby Fischer, Boris Spassky, and Gary Kasparov, all set against the exotic backdrop of Thailand's capital city? Brilliant!

"One Night in Bangkok" starts with the innocuous sounds of an orchestra tuning up, which soon give way to a dark, driving 90-second instrumental piece full of urgency and Cold War intrigue, and then—*bang!*—in jumps Murray Head singing with manic enthusiasm about everyone and everything from Somerset Maugham to massage parlors to Yul Brynner to Iceland to queens on a chess board. One line to the next, the listener hasn't a clue where the tune is heading, and it's a rare single, indeed, that would've benefited by an accompanying set of Cliffs Notes to explain the myriad cultural references.

Although "One Night in Bangkok" remains Murray Head's only Top 40 hit as purely a solo act, the Englishman did reach #14 back in 1971 with a track called "Superstar," which was featured in the rock opera *Jesus Christ Superstar*. Those who owned "Superstar" on 45 might recall that the label listed the artist as *Murray Head with The Trinidad Singers*. Head actually played Judas in the original London production of *Jesus Christ Superstar*, with Ian Gillan of Deep Purple as Jesus and Yvonne "If I Can't Have You" Elliman taking the role of Mary Magdalene.

While Murray Head gave voice to "One Night in Bangkok," the song was written by Benny Andersson, Bjorn Ulvaeus, and Tim Rice. Messrs. Andersson and Ulvaeus are, of course, well known as two of the founding members of ABBA, while Rice, or should we say Sir Tim, as he was knighted by the Queen in 1994, is renowned for his many collaborations with Andrew Lloyd Weber, including *Joseph and the Amazing Technicolor Dreamcoat*, the aforementioned *Jesus Christ Superstar*, and *Evita*.

Finally, it's often erroneously believed that "One Night in Bangkok" initially appeared as part of Tim Rice's musical *Chess*, but in ac-

---

Take a straight and stronger course to the corner of your life / Make the White Queen run so fast, she hasn't got time to make you a wife.
                                        —"Your Move" by Yes, 1971

The London prog-rockers Yes charted six times, with "Roundabout" (#13 in '72) and "Owner of a Lonely Heart" (#1 in '83) being their most well-known tunes. The outfit's first hit, however, was "Your Move," which spent two weeks at #40 in December of '71. The fascinating and unusual thing about "Your Move" was that, like "One Night in Bangkok," the song used the game of chess as a metaphor for various aspects of everyday life.

tual fact, this show didn't open in London's West End until a good two years after the release of a concept album also called *Chess*. So, the song really became a #3 smash based on its release as a single off the *Chess* LP, rather than its subsequent exposure in the musical of the same name.

#42

"How Long" by Ace, 1975

But I can't help but have my suspicion
'Cause I ain't quite as dumb as I seem

Peaked nationally at #3
Lead singer: Paul Carrack
Written by Paul Carrack

The story of the group Ace is really the tale of a talented Englishman named Paul Carrack, as he both wrote and sang lead on "How Long," the outfit's only hit record.

Paul Carrack is easily one of pop music's most intriguing, accomplished figures. Just examine a small portion of the guy's resume: lead singer of Ace; lead singer of Mike + the Mechanics; lead singer on Squeeze's "Tempted"; briefly worked with Roxy Music; and Top 10 solo act ("Don't Shed a Tear," #9 in 1988). Funny thing is, Carrack could walk down any street in America (or, for that matter, his native Britain) and dollars to doughnuts, not a single person would recognize him. It doesn't happen often in today's star-obsessed, need-to-know-every-detail society, but Paul Carrack is that rare person who could accurately be described as both famous *and* unknown.

At its heart and soul, "How Long" is the quintessential bar-band number—straight-ahead, no-frills rock 'n' roll. Like "Smoke from a Distant Fire" by The Sanford/Townsend Band, another classic one-hitter from the 70s, this song doesn't need to rely on synthesizers, drum machines, or slick post-production tricks. No, "How Long" sticks to the basics: a chugging bass line complemented by precise, Steely Dan–ish lead guitar and, of course, flawless vocals. You hear Carrack on Mike + the Mechanics' "All I Need Is a Miracle," and you think to yourself, "Man, there's a guy with a clear, strong voice." Then you catch him on "Silent Running (On Dangerous Ground)," and he impresses you with an earnest soulfulness, even adding a touch of gospel to round out his delivery. But none of this prepares you for Carrack's work on "How Long," which has to be considered among the all-time best lead vocals in pop history. His voice is smooth, powerful, and a touch bluesy, plus he does something highly unusual for a rocker: He subtly bends and swings his words, especially coming out of the guitar break midway through the track. The overall sound is part Boz Scaggs, part Daryl Hall, with perhaps a hint of Michael McDonald and Christopher Cross added to the mix.

During Ace's five-year run, 1972 through 1977, the band released three albums: *Five-a-Side, Time for Another,* and *No Strings,* none of which remains in print. "How Long" appeared on their first LP. Interestingly, a cover version of the Carrack-penned tune was done by the Minneapolis funksters Lipps, Inc., of all artists, the one-hit wonders remembered (some would say fondly, others would say not so fondly) for the #1 smash "Funkytown" back in 1980. Bobby Womack and Rod Stewart have also covered "How Long."

Ace is, of course, long gone. However, Carrack, based out of Hertfordshire, England, just north of London, is very much alive and well

In 1928, nearly a half-century before Paul Carrack and "Ace" scored a Top 5 with "How Long," Leroy Carr, a fellow living in Indianapolis, wrote a song called "How Long, How Long Blues," which became a hit for Carr and his musical partner, Scrapper Blackwell.

and making terrific music. Over the years, he's issued more than a dozen solo albums, including the cleverly named *Ace Mechanic* and *Carrackter Reference*. Paul Carrack also tours regularly with his own band, performing mainly in Germany and the United Kingdom.

#41

"Kiss Me Deadly" by Lita Ford, 1988

I went to a party last Saturday night
I didn't get laid, I got in a fight

Peaked nationally at #12
Lead singer: Lita Ford
Written by Mick Smiley

"Kiss Me Deadly" boasts the earthiest opening lines in pop history: "I went to a party last Saturday night / I didn't get laid, I got in a fight." How can you beat that?! Over the years, thousand of songs have circled the issue, talking about "making love" or *not* making love, "gettin' it on," "doin' the wild thing," and every other euphemism under the sun, but only one tune unabashedly came right out and uttered the dreaded word "laid." Hey, to paraphrase Jimmy Buffet: The chick just wanted to have a few drinks and screw. The fact that she ended up in a scuffle instead, well, you know, these things happen.

Kip Winger. Night Ranger. Jon Bon Jovi. Poison. David Lee Roth. Def Leppard. Whitesnake. And then there was Lita Ford, pretty much the lone female playing among the boys in the hair/pop metal sandbox of the 80s. Sure, there were other women like Pat Benatar and Joan Jett, Ford's former bandmate in The Runaways, rocking out during that same period, but only Lita, who was sometimes referred to as "The Queen of Noise," went full throttle.

In 1988, a year that spawned The Beach Boys' sipping-pink-drinks-by-the-pool tune "Kokomo," Bobby McFerrin's goofy "Don't Worry Be Happy," and "She's Like the Wind" by Patrick "Dirty Dancing" Swayze, "Kiss Me Deadly" delivered a shot of some much-needed rock 'n' roll adrenaline to the Top 40. The song was all buzzing guitars, pounding drums, and of course, Ford's loud, clear, blue-collar voice. Partying, trying to get lucky, cadging a ten-spot from the "old man," running late for work, downing a couple of brewskies, kissing, and dancing—in just about exactly four minutes, the record captured the hopes and frustrations of being a working-class kid.

"Kiss Me Deadly" originally appeared on the *Lita* album. Subsequently, the tune has been included on no fewer than four Lita Ford "best of" compilations. You really hate to be jaded and cynical, especially because "Kiss Me Deadly" is such a terrific track, but, come on, *one* hit single, *four* full-blown "greatest hits" releases? Yes, Mistress Lita also landed at #8 in the spring of '89 with "Close My Eyes Forever," however, that was as part of a duet with Ozzy Osbourne. Her chart success strictly as a solo act began and ended with "Kiss Me Deadly."

Today, some 15 years after her moment in hair metal heaven, when she was winning *Guitar* magazine's award as Best Female Guitarist and taking her *Lita* CD platinum, Ford lives with her husband, Jim Gillette, and their young son, James Leonard. By the way, before marrying Gillette, Lita Ford was briefly married to a guy named Chris Holmes, the guitarist in a Southern California band called W.A.S.P. Devotees of 80s heavy metal will recall that W.A.S.P. stood for We Are Sexual Perverts, which is basically all the ammunition you need the next time you're having a friendly argument with your buddies about whether or not the movie *Spinal Tap* was, in fact, based on reality.

Brent's Two Cents: The video for "Kiss Me Deadly" is almost beyond description, but I'll give it a go. Okay, first of all, Lita Ford wears a black leather bustier throughout the proceedings, and her blonde hair is positively Farrah Fawcett circa 1977. The set appears to be a darkened underground parking garage that's been decorated with huge blocks of ice and random cauldrons of fire. It's against this backdrop that Ford slinks and struts through her hit single.

The highlight of the entire video—and this is a genuine *Beavis & Butt-head* moment—comes about ninety seconds in when Lita Ford drops to the ground with an eye toward, how should I put this politely, *humping* her electric guitar, and in knee pads no less! Just good, wholesome entertainment for the entire family.

#40

"Breakfast at Tiffany's" by Deep Blue Something, 1995

And I said, "What about Breakfast at Tiffany's?"
She said, "I think I remember the film"

Peaked nationally at #5
Lead singer: Todd Pipes
Written by Todd Pipes

Deep Purple? No, Deep Blue . . . Something. Rock 'n' roll legend has it that back in 1993, when this quartet from Denton, Texas, was brainstorming, trying to come up with a cool name for their new band, they decided it had to be called Deep Blue something or another. Deep Blue Butterfly? Nah, too Sixties. Deep Blue Happiness? Nope, that doesn't work. Deep Blue Asphalt? Noooo. Ah, the heck with it, let's just go with Deep Blue Something. And so the unusual moniker was born.

"Breakfast at Tiffany's," Deep Blue Something's lone hit single, spent an impressive 26 weeks in the Top 40, reaching as high as #5. If you were tuned to the FM dial in late '95 or early '96, there was no escaping it. The fascinating thing about this record, and perhaps the

The same year, 1995, that Deep Blue Something scored with "Breakfast at Tiffany's," a group called Deep Banana Blackout formed to play their own brand of Tower of Power–esque pop-funk. The 90s also saw the emergence of such "deep" bands as Deep Puddle Dynamics, The Deep Fried Clams, Deeper Than Space, and Deeper Side of London. Of course, going back to the late 70s and early 80s, there was Deep Freeze Mice, the punksters who gave us the crazily named album *My Geraniums Are Bulletproof*. And, finally, let's not forget Deep River Boys, the R&B outfit that enjoyed tremendous popularity in the 40s and 50s.

exact reason why it enjoyed such a long stay on the charts, was that it never really seemed to be anyone's favorite tune, yet, at the same time, no one disliked it. You might say that "Breakfast at Tiffany's" wore well. It was just kind of *there* for six months, certainly not setting the music world on fire, but not getting on radio listeners' nerves, either.

All acoustic guitar and straightforward, earnest lyrics, "Breakfast at Tiffany's" was very much a product of its time, that post-grunge, mid-90s era that gave us tracks like "Counting Blue Cars" by Dishwalla, "Hand in My Pocket" by Alanis Morissette, and Third Eye Blind's "How's It Going to Be." Of course, the most memorable part of Deep Blue Something's song might have been the accompanying video, which was shot right on Manhattan's Fifth Avenue in front of Tiffany & Co., Holly Golightly's favorite early morning noshing spot.

Home, the album from which "Breakfast at Tiffany's" was culled, was issued in the summer of 1995; however, it wasn't until spring of 2001 that the Texans released their next compact disc, *Deep Blue Something*. From a music biz standpoint, one word springs to mind: mistake! Mind you, the group said they wanted to let *Home* "run its course." Guys, that CD ran its course before Bill Clinton began his second term. Which explains Deep Blue Something's status as one-hit wonders. If you're lucky and talented enough to capture the nation's attention with a Top 10 smash, for the love of Pete, keep the momentum going by hustling out a strong follow-up. Even the mailroom clerk at Interscope Records can tell you that six years between albums is a career killer.

Today, Deep Blue Something is signed to the Aezra label out of Phoenix, and the band occasionally plays live gigs at places like Joe's in Chicago, Studio Movie Grill in Plano, Texas, and Dallas's Club Clearview.

#39

"A Little Bit of Soap" by The Jarmels, 1961

A little bit of soap
Will never wash away my tears

Peaked nationally at #12
Lead singer: Paul Burnett
Written by Bert Russell

The Jarmels were composed of Paul Burnett, Earl Christian, Tom Eldridge, Nathaniel Ruff, and Ray Smith. The group formed in Richmond, Virginia, in 1959, but found their greatest success recording out of New York City in the very early 60s.

The story of The Jarmels and "A Little Bit of Soap" is, in many ways, the story of Bert Berns, the fellow who penned the outfit's lone hit record under the name Bert Russell. Berns, who died in 1967 at the age of 38, was an unsung, behind-the-scenes pop pioneer, a genuine creative genius who, even during the height of his career, could have walked down Seventh Avenue during the lunchtime pedestrian rush without drawing so much as even a single glance. While his face might not have been recognizable, Bert Berns's music unquestionably was. Consider this for a *curriculum vitae*: he co-wrote "Hang on Sloopy," which The McCoys rode all the way to #1 in 1965; he co-wrote "Twist and Shout," of Isley Brothers and Beatles fame; he wrote "Here Comes the Night," recorded by Van Morrison and his band Them; he co-wrote "Piece of My Heart," a cooker driven to #12 back in '68 by Big Brother & the Holding Company, featuring Janis Joplin; and, of course, he wrote "A Little Bit of Soap."

Today, more than 40 years after its release, The Jarmels' take on "A Little Bit of Soap" sounds fresh and relevant. Paul Burnett's confident lead vocals, so beautifully clear and soulful, are really what make this tune so memorable. Burnett sings with just a hint of a cry in his voice that suits the material perfectly. By the way, when Britisher Nigel Olsson covered "A Little Bit of Soap," peaking at #34 in '79, that *cry* was largely absent, much to the track's detriment. And, surprisingly, Olsson's version, while post-dating The Jarmels' by almost 20 years, has not aged nearly as well as the original. In fact, only the strangely named Showaddywaddy, a band out of Leicester, England, that enjoyed tremendous popularity in the U.K. during the 70s and 80s, has ever managed to capture on wax the subtle plaintiveness displayed in 1961 by Paul Burnett and his mates.

Interestingly, a full-length Jarmels album was never pressed dur-

From the darkly atmospheric instrumental "Apache" by Denmark's Jorgen Ingmann to Ernie K-Doe's humorous "Mother-in-Law," The Jarmels enjoyed good one-hit wonder company during 1961. The year John and Jacqueline Kennedy moved into 1600 Pennsylvania Avenue also found Philco transistor radios picking up "Peanut Butter" by The Marathons, Arthur Lyman's "Yellowbird," and "Who Put the Bomp (In the Bomp, Bomp, Bomp)" by Barry Mann, all memorable one-hitters.

ing the 60s. All of the group's music, including "A Little Bit of Soap," was released exclusively on 45s; however, in the mid-90s, Collectables Records issued *14 Golden Classics: Jarmels*, a CD that featured the only 14 tracks The Jarmels ever laid down in the studio. Also, over the years, "A Little Bit of Soap" has naturally found its way onto numerous Oldies compilations, among them *Hi-Fi Rock 'n' Roll Party, Cruisin',* and *Radio Gold.*

Sadly, all of The Jarmels save for Ray Smith, who, incidentally, is a minister, have passed away. However, Messrs. Burnett, Christian, Eldridge, and Ruff, along with, of course, Bert Berns, continue to live on in pop music spirit whenever a WCBS-FM in New York City or a Majic 102.7 in Miami spin "A Little Bit of Soap."

#38

"More Than Just the Two of Us" by Sneaker, 1982

It's more than just the two of us
And we just have to keep holding on, holding on

Peaked nationally at #34
Lead singer: Mitch Crane
Written by Mitch Crane and Michael Carey Schneider

If "More Than Just the Two of Us" were playing on the jukebox at your local Bennigan's, everyone in the place born after, say, 1968 would, if only somewhat vaguely, recognize the song. Hardly anyone, though, could name the artist: Sneaker.

The group took their name from a Steely Dan track called "Bad Sneakers," which appeared on Messrs. Fagen and Becker's *Katy Lied* LP. In fact, Jeff "Skunk" Baxter, who played lead guitar with Steely Dan in the 70s, acted as Sneaker's producer.

Sneaker, operating out of Southern California, was composed of Michael Cottage, Mitch Crane, Mike Hughes, Jim King, Michael Carey Schneider, and Tim Torrance. The outfit released only two albums: *Sneaker* and *Loose in the World*, their lone hit appearing on the former.

"More Than Just the Two of Us" is an exceptionally well-crafted piece of music. That the tune only reached as high as #34 remains a head-scratcher, as this is solid, Top 10 material. The cut starts with a sad, slow, 23-second instrumental introduction, setting the tone for the entire record, which is decidedly melancholy. Vocally, this cut is superb: Crane's clear, yet somewhat downcast, lead is complemented beautifully by lush, dreamy background harmonies. The lyrics, however, are the most intriguing aspect of "More Than Just the Two of Us." The exact message of this record is inscrutable, which is not usually the case with 80s pop. Sure, at one level, it's a classic, straightforward love song about the deep bond between two people, but then there's this allusion to vague, unnamed forces that are pulling at these lovers, which adds a measure of struggle and desperation to the proceedings. For this very reason, it's curious that "More Than Just the Two of Us" has joined the likes of Edwin McCain's "Could Not Ask for More" and "We've Only Just Begun" by The Carpenters as wedding reception favorites. While Sneaker's single is exceptionally

---

sneaker (*noun*) a usually canvas sports shoe with a pliable rubber sole.

In addition to the classic one-hitters Sneaker, the music world has also seen The Sneakers, power popsters from North Carolina who issued two albums, 1978's *In the Red* and *Racket* from 1992. Then, there was The Sneaker, purveyors of electronica who gave us the *Scatterbomb* CD in 1999. Finally, let's not forget Sneaker Pimps, the trip hoppers from England known for songs like "Post-Modern Sleaze," "Low Place Like Home," and "Spin Spin Sugar," all taken from the *Becoming X* LP.

atmospheric, one can't help but believe joyous, fresh-faced brides and grooms across America might be missing its inherent sadness.

After "More Than Just the Two of Us" cracked the Top 40, "Don't Let Me In," another cut off the *Sneaker* album, was released—to no effect, though, as the track ran out of gas at #63. "Don't Let Me In," however, was written by the aforementioned Steely Dan duo of Donald Fagen and Walter Becker, a pedigree that rescues the song from complete obscurity.

Interestingly, in 2001, a Sneaker compact disc called *Early On* was issued in Japan. This CD contained recordings from the group's embryonic stages, and "More Than Just the Two of Us" was not among them.

#37

"Black Velvet" by Alannah Myles, 1990

Mississippi in the middle of a dry spell
Jimmy Rogers on the Victrola up high

Peaked nationally at #1
Lead singer: Alannah Myles
Written by David Tyson and Christopher Ward

"Black Velvet," a song dripping in Americana, was actually recorded in Toronto, Canada, where one-hitter Alannah Myles has made her home at various times over the years. And before our friends up in Ontario start with the cries of "Alannah had *two* American hits," let's coolly examine the facts. Yes, Myles's "Love Is" did creep into the Top 40, peaking at #36, but, c'mon, after having a #1 smash, your follow-up simply must perform better than #36 to save you from one-hit wonderdom. Just ask Nu Shooz, a-ha, Looking Glass, and The Dream Academy.

The singer was born Alannah Byles on Christmas Day of 1955. Her father, the late Bill Byles, was a 1997 inductee into the Canadian Broadcast Hall of Fame, so it's not surprising that his daughter pursued a career in the entertainment field. What is puzzling, though, is that Myles never became a hit machine after her huge success with "Black Velvet." However, if you take the time to listen, even casually, to *Alannah Myles*, the album from which her famous single was taken, you can easily recognize what stood between Myles and a string of chart toppers: her sound is unsatisfyingly all over the musical map. "Black Velvet" is a bluesy, twangy, honky-tonk rocker, and it works marvelously. You're thinking, "Way to go, Alannah—give us more of that!" But then, you hear a tune like "Kick Start My Heart" coming across as third-rate Joan Jett, and it totally harshes the vibe. Follow that with ersatz Stevie Nicks in the form of "Just One Kiss" and, well, it's just not happening on the FM dial for Ms. Myles.

Of course, some music biz pundits have posited that even if Alannah Myles had pumped out more tracks in the vein of "Black Velvet," it still wouldn't have mattered because the 1990s proved an especially inhospitable period for that brand of countrified pop. The critics maintained that her #1 record was a fluke. Sure, she caught lightning in a bottle once, they said, but it wasn't the sort of success that could be replicated, and certainly not during the 90s. The so-called musical "experts," however, did a one-hundred-eighty-degree about-face later in the decade when another pretty Canadian song-stress, Shania Twain, blitzed the Top 40 with no fewer than seven songs, including "You're Still the One," "That Don't Impress Me Much," and "Man! I Feel Like a Woman!" Admittedly, Twain's style was brighter and less sultry than what Myles employed on "Black Velvet," but both singers brought more than a little Memphis and Nashville to the charts, so with the benefit of 20/20 hindsight, it's clear Alannah Myles would have been better served had she stuck with that winning formula.

Even though she has failed to become a household name, rest assured that Alanis Morissette, Sarah McLachlan, and Joni Mitchell won't be planning a benefit for their fellow countrywoman anytime

soon. Myles has sold millions of albums worldwide throughout a career that is still showing a steady pulse. Indeed, she continues recording to this day on the Ark 21 record label, which is run by Miles
Copeland, brother of Stewart Copeland of Police fame.

Brent's Two Cents: The thing I like best about Alannah Myles is her
honest, shoot-from-the-hip attitude. Here is what she had to say on
the topic of why she definitely would *not* want to take part in the
much-hyped Lilith Fair: "I don't want to be with a bunch of these
chicks; half of them can't sing and half of them just have record company money and they're there because they're famous and the
hottest items and happen to be women. I think it's disgusting."

   The Very Best of Alannah Myles on compact disc: $16.95. Alannah
Myles's dissing of the self-important Lilith Fair participants: priceless.

#36

"Romeo's Tune" by Steve Forbert, 1980

Meet me in the middle of the day
Let me hear you say everything's okay

Peaked nationally at #11
Lead singer: Steve Forbert
Written by Steve Forbert

Jonathan Yardley of *The Washington Post* once wrote of Steve Forbert:
"The impression he's made on American culture is so small as to be
almost invisible. To put it another (and quite deliberately provocative)
way, If Bob Dylan were any good, he'd be Steve Forbert."

   "Disco Duck" by Rick Dees & His Cast of Idiots reached #1 in
1976. Australia's Air Supply landed 11 singles on the charts. Debby

Boone's "You Light Up My Life" spent nearly six months in the Top 40. If Steve Forbert were, right at this very minute, sitting alone at a smoky bar in his native Meridian, Mississippi, throwing down another Jack Black, no one could blame the man. However, throughout his career, the abundantly talented Forbert, the guy who the music intelligentsia once dubbed "the next Bob Dylan," has been far too determined and self-assured to let a relative lack of commercial success get the better of him.

"Romeo's Tune," Forbert's lone charter, comes off his second album, *Jackrabbit Slim*. Like "Someday, Someway" by fellow one-hitter Marshall Crenshaw, this song, starting with Note One, positively springs from the speakers with a bright, fresh energy. Indeed, "Romeo's Tune's" 20-second introduction, with its sunshiny, kinetic keyboard riff, is among the most distinctive and memorable in pop history. And Forbert's voice, all clear and soulful, with a slight hint of Southern gospel, fits the material perfectly. Of course, another cool thing about this record is its somewhat enigmatic title: "Romeo's Tune." Nowhere to be found in the track's three minutes and twenty-nine seconds is the word *Romeo*. It's akin to that Rod Stewart hit from the early 80s called "Young Turks," wherein the tousled-haired Scotsman never once utters the actual phrase "young turks."

When Steve Forbert arrived in New York City at the age of 21 and put up at a Manhattan YMCA, he must have felt a million miles away from his Mississippi home, especially when he took to busking in the cold, cavernous hallways of Grand Central Terminal for quarters and dimes. On his first album, *Alive on Arrival*, Forbert eloquently expressed his thoughts about being a newcomer alone in The Nitty Gritty City in the form of songs like "Tonight I Feel So Far Away from Home" and "Grand Central Station, March 18, 1977." In fact, the latter tune is perhaps the finest ever written about trying to make it and keeping a stiff upper lip in the face of what, at times, seems like the world's cruel indifference to one's ambitions. You listen to "Grand Central Station..." a handful of times and only the most hard-hearted among us wouldn't want to reach back in time to that March 18th day in the late 70s so we could give young Steve an encouraging smile while dropping a buck into his battered guitar case.

These days, Steve Forbert soldiers on, playing dozens of live shows every year at small- to medium-sized clubs across America—places like The Bottom Line in New York's Greenwich Village, Berkeley's Freight and Salvage, The Ark in Ann Arbor, and Philadelphia's Tin Angel. As for CDs, Forbert has released 15 so far, including 1997's *Here's Your Pizza*, which boasts one of the most creative album covers ever.

Brent's Two Cents: "Romeo's Tune" is a terrific song; however, I believe a couple of cuts that never even caught a glimpse of the Top 40, "Goin' Down to Laurel" and "Steve Forbert's Midsummer Night's Toast," are just as good.

By the way, it's been reported over the years that Forbert dedicated "Romeo's Tune" to Florence Ballard, the late member of The Supremes. There does, however, seem to be some confusion regarding this assertion. Consider what the singer from Mississippi said to music journalist Kevin Conley when asked about whether or not there was a "Romeo's Tune"–Ballard connection: "Yes, in the [Supremes] song 'Back in My Arms, Again,' the boy she loves is a Romeo. At that time, Florence had died in the ghetto, in Detroit, totally broke. That seemed like such a tragedy, so I dedicated the song ['Romeo's Tune'] to her." On the other hand, read what Bill Ellis wrote in the January 22, 2000, edition of the *Memphis Commercial Appeal* after interviewing Steve Forbert: "He also swears the song ['Romeo's Tune'] isn't about Supremes singer Florence Ballard, who died destitute at age 32 in 1976. Forbert admits that Ballard became a timely connection for 'Romeo's Tune,' written about a girl from Meridian."

#35

"Brandy (You're a Fine Girl)" by Looking Glass, 1972

Brandy wears a braided chain
Made of finest silver from the north of Spain

Peaked nationally at #1
Lead singer: Elliot Lurie
Written by Elliot Lurie

"Brandy (You're a Fine Girl)" belongs in a category all by itself. Name another pop song that could properly be called a somewhat bluesy/jazzy, Top 40 sea chantey. Elliot Lurie's vocal is what really makes this record go. Although it sounds like a contradiction, his voice manages to be simultaneously husky, crisp, and lazy. If you listen closely to "Brandy," you can hear traces of Neil Diamond's "Cracklin' Rosie." Incidentally, like the more famous Diamond, Lurie was born in Brooklyn. As with many of the best one-hit wonders, "Brandy" has legs. This tune shows absolutely no signs of fading from the pop culture landscape. In addition to being a staple on Oldies stations from Miami to Minneapolis, "Brandy" is no stranger to Hollywood either, having been featured in such movies as *Charlie's Angels* and *A Very Brady Sequel*. Pretty good for a song that started its life thirty years ago as a throwaway B-side to a 45 r.p.m. that presented the unknown single "Don't It Make You Feel Good" as the hit side.

Of course, true chart sticklers don't consider Looking Glass to be a one-hit wonder at all. A year after "Brandy" spent 14 weeks in the Top 40, zooming clear past every other record to capture the #1 spot, the band charted with a second single called "Jimmy Loves Mary-Anne." This obscure tune peaked at #33, and fell off the charts in less than a month. So, Looking Glass is, technically, a two-hitter. However, the next person who tells you they remember "Jimmy Loves Mary-Anne" will probably be the first—and last.

Looking Glass issued only three albums: *Looking Glass, Brandy,* and *Subway Serenade.* The first two were released in 1972, the third in 1973, and all three are long out of print. However, in the late 90s, the CDs *Golden Classics* and *Brandy (You're a Fine Girl)* were brought to market in an attempt to catch the ears of those who remember a time when pop/rock music was actually heard up and down the AM dial.

By the way, when "Brandy (You're a Fine Girl)" reached #1 in the summer of '72, do you recall what single was nipping at its heels at #2? Gilbert O'Sullivan's "Alone Again (Naturally)." Never underestimate the power of parentheses in a song's title.

Brent's Two Cents: I was 11 years old in 1972, living in the town of Framingham, Massachusetts, and I can vividly remember WRKO-AM in Boston spinning Looking Glass's "Brandy" over and over again that year. I mean, there were days during summer vacation when I swear I must have heard that song played on RKO at least six, seven, eight times, maybe more. And I loved it each time, as did my older brother, Kyle. In fact, until he discovered Steely Dan's "Reelin' in the Years" over on the mysterious FM band, "Brandy" was Kyle's favorite tune.

No doubt about it, with my pink plastic General Electric AM radio hidden under the pillow at night for surreptitious Top 40 listening, 1972 was the year I began a lifelong fascination with pop music. That was three decades ago, yet I can still easily recall many classic one-hit singles from '72, records like "Day by Day" (Godspell), "Hot Rod Lincoln" (Commander Cody & His Lost Planet Airmen), "How Do You Do?" (Mouth & MacNeal), "Popcorn" (Hot Butter), "Precious and Few" (Climax), "Sunshine" (Jonathan Edwards), and "Thunder and Lightning" (Chi Coltrane).

#34

"99 Luftballons" by Nena, 1984/
"99 Red Balloons" (English version)

Floating in the summer sky
Ninety-nine red balloons go by

Peaked nationally at #2
Lead singer: Gabriele Kerner
Written by Uwe Fahrenkrog-Petersen and Carlo Karges
English version written by Kevin McAlea

Nena was a New Wave band from Berlin composed of Gabriele Kerner, Carlo Karges, Uwe Fahrenkrog-Petersen, Jurgen Dehmel, and Rolf Brendel. Gabriele Kerner, the outfit's founder and lead singer, was nicknamed "Nena," hence the group's name.

This was an unusual song in that two separate versions by Nena, one in German ("99 Luftballons"), the other in English ("99 Red Balloons"), received major radio airplay simultaneously. Surprisingly, it was the German language single that charted. And while the instrumental tracks for "99 Luftballons" and "99 Red Balloons" were virtually identical, the lyrics differed. Many assumed that what they heard in English was more or less a direct, literal translation of the original *Deutsche. Nein!* Starting with their titles—99 *air* balloons versus 99 *red* balloons—the tunes diverged markedly on a lyrical level. Yes, at their core, both records carried the same Reagan-era anti-nuclear message, yet the German version is somewhat darker and more politically pointed than the English.

Along with a-ha's "Take on Me" and Dexys Midnight Runners' "Come on Eileen," probably no other one-hitter is more associated with the 80s than "99 Red Balloons." In fact, when the director of *The*

Wedding Singer—the quintessential look back at the decade that spawned MTV, Air Jordan sneakers, and *Miami Vice*—wanted the perfect visual shorthand for that period, he simply shot a few seconds of Drew Barrymore, stereo headphones in place, blissfully bopping to Nena's #2 smash.

For a track that is 20 years old, "99 Luftballons" continues to capture musical imaginations worldwide. Indeed, the song has in all likelihood been covered more times, and certainly with more diversity, than any other one-hit wonder from the 80s or 90s. It's been waxed by everyone from Icelandic songstress Bjork to the Mexican group Timbiriche to the Southern California ska-punskters Goldfinger to Bao Han, the female singer from Vietnam. By the way, the aforementioned Timbiriche's version (sung entirely in Spanish) is called "Mi Globo Azul," which means "My Blue Balloon." Amazingly, even that master of 60s easy listening, Mr. Ray Conniff, took a crack at "99 Red Balloons" on his *Campeones* CD from 1985.

Between 1983 and 1986, Nena released seven albums as a full-fledged band. Then from 1989 through 2002, Gabriele Kerner, recording as a solo act under the Nena banner, issued more than a dozen compact discs, many of which were geared toward children. Kerner has also been a fixture on German television over the years, even acting as host of a live program called *Metro*.

Going back to the 1950s, continental Europe has spawned a passel of memorable one-hit wonders. Germany gave us Nena ("99 Luftballons"), Horst Jankowski ("A Walk In the Black Forest"), and Harold Faltermeyer ("Axel F"). From Norway, we had a-ha ("Take on Me") and Jorgen Ingmann & His Guitar ("Apache"). Domenico Modugno ("Volare [Nel Blu Dipinto di Blu]") sprang from Italy. Bent Fabric ("Alley Cat") was from Denmark. From Belgium came The Singing Nun ("Dominique"). And, finally, let's not forget Mouth & MacNeal ("How Do You Do?") of The Netherlands.

#33

"California Sun" by The Rivieras, 1964

Well, they're out there a' havin' fun
In that warm California sun

Peaked nationally at #5
Lead singer: Marty Fortson
Written by Henry Glover and Morris Levy

The Rivieras hailed from South Bend, Indiana, which is rather surprising for a band that waxed the quintessential West Coast, fun-in-the-sun, rock 'n' roll record. Rust Belt surf, you might call it.

"California Sun" was first recorded by Joe Jones, a New Orleans rocker and one-hit wonder known for "You Talk Too Much," which reached #3 in 1960. However, it took five Hoosier high schoolers to put the song on the national map. The Rivieras, who originally dubbed themselves The Playmates, were composed of Marty Fortson, Joe Pennell, Doug Gean, Paul Dennert, and Otto Nuss. This initial lineup, however, was short lived, as Fortson and Pennell, the lead singer and lead guitarist, respectively, decided to join the Marines soon after taking part in the "California Sun" recording session at a studio in nearby Chicago. Over the years, Marty Fortson has spoken about the strange sensation of hearing his singing voice coming out over Armed Forces Radio as he was dodging bullets in Southeast Asia. Given this rather uneasy association between Fortson's military experience and his vocal turn on The Rivieras' #5 smash, it's interesting to note that "California Sun" was prominently featured in the movie *Good Morning, Vietnam*, in which, of course, Robin Williams played Adrian Cronauer, an Armed Forces Radio disk jockey.

While Fortson and Pennell were busy serving their Uncle Sam, a revamped Rivieras, with a Top 10 hit on their hands, began touring the United States, opening for British Invasion acts like The Dave

Clark Five and The Kinks. Ironically, it was the arrival of this wave of Englishmen on American shores and airwaves, more than any other factor, that contributed to the boys from South Bend being recalled today as one-hit wonders. Just as "California Sun" was gaining steam in the winter of '64, along came John, Paul, George, and Ringo with a suitcase chock full of "I Want to Hold Your Hand," "She Loves You," and "Please Please Me." Game over! The Rivieras would issue a handful of follow-up singles, none of which managed to do better than #93, and the outfit that had begun with such youthful energy and promise called it a day in 1966.

Interestingly, during the 80s and 90s, "California Sun" became a staple in the repertoire of numerous high-profile punk bands. Everyone from The Ramones to Rancid to The Vindictives did their own three-chord take on the tune, drawn as they were to its solid, simple roots of rock 'n' roll structure.

These days, three of the original members, Marty Fortson, Otto Nuss, and Doug Gean, continue performing on occasion under The Rivieras banner, often at private parties, corporate functions, and outdoor summer festivals. In 2000, two career retrospective compact discs, *The Best of The Rivieras: California Sun* and *Let's Stomp with The Rivieras*, were released on Norton Records, exposing a whole new generation to that Midwestern-style warm California sun.

What do the Spencer Davis Group, Silver Convention, and Maxine Nightingale have in common? They were all *two*-hit wonders. Back in 1967, Spencer Davis scored with "Gimme Some Lovin'" at #7 and "I'm a Man" at #10. Silver Convention, a band out of Munich, Germany, landed at #1 in 1975 with "Fly, Robin, Fly." A year later, they earned a #2 with "Get Up and Boogie (That's Right)." As for Ms. Nightingale, she had "Right Back Where We Started From," a #2 in 1976, as well as the #5 "Lead Me On" in 1979.

#32

"Breakout" by Swing Out Sister, 1987

The time has come to make or break
Move on, don't hesitate—breakout!

Peaked nationally at #6
Lead singer: Corrine Drewery
Written by Swing Out Sister

The first track on Tom Waits's CD *Mule Variations* is called "Big in Japan." The third cut on Alphaville's *Forever Young* album: "Big in Japan." Swing Out Sister has never recorded a song by that name, but those three words—"big in Japan"—provide valuable insight into the group's status as one-hit wonders. More on Swing Out Sister's connection to the Land of the Rising Sun later.

For, oh, perhaps ten minutes in the late 80s, mainstream radio listeners and record buyers came down with a sudden, inexplicable case of good taste and sophistication in pop music. It passed quickly, though, and no lasting damage was done. But for a brief, golden moment right around the time that the Gipper was handing over the castle keys to George Bush I, the Danny Wilsons, Basias, and Swing Out Sisters of the world gave us a taste of what could be, if only we'd open our ears and be willing to expand our musical horizons beyond Bon Jovi and Paula Abdul.

The original Swing Out Sister lineup was Corrine Drewery, Andy Connell, and Martin Jackson, and they hailed from Manchester, England's Second City. The band purveyed a brand of stylish, jazz-tinged pop that, outside of Steely Dan, has seldom enjoyed any chart success. Their Top 10 smash, "Breakout," was all brassy horns and cool, sleek vocals, and to suggest that the tune stood out from, say, Whitesnake's "Hear I Go Again," well, the phrase "laughable understatement" comes to mind. By the way, the group took their name from

Swing Out, Sister, a 1945 British film starring Arthur Treacher and Billie Burke.

Unlike other one-hit smashes from the 1980s such as "Come on Eileen," "Life in a Northern Town," and "Take on Me," which still get aired constantly on the FM dial often as part of a *Saturday Night at the 80s* or an *All Request 80s Lunch* type of program, "Breakout" has largely been forgotten by the radio. In New York City, for instance, only CD-101, a so-called Smooth Jazz station, still plays Swing Out Sister's hit from 1987. Therein lies the reason why the Mancunian trio never was able to duplicate their early success on the pop charts: they were too jazzy. Ironically, America, the birthplace of jazz, doesn't like the genre—in fact, only two percent of the music sold in this country is jazz. And, even when jazz is leavened with pop to make it more accessible and palatable, mainstream Americans come to the buffet table, curiously nibble at a "Time and Tide" by Basia or a "Breakout," kind of indifferently shrug their shoulders, and move on.

However, in Osaka and Fukuoka, it's an entirely different story, and this gets back to Swing Out Sister being "big in Japan." Corrine Drewery and Andy Connell (the group is now a duo) are, in fact, household names in Nippon, spending about four months a year touring the country, often with a 10-piece backing band. Indeed, Swing Out Sister's "Now You're Not Here" was even used as the theme song for *The Midday Moon*, a popular Japanese television show, and based on the wide exposure from that TV program, the record even earned Drewery and Connell a Grand Prix award, which is essentially a Japanese Grammy. So, while recent Swing Out Sister offerings such as *Filth and Dreams* and *Somewhere Deep in the Night* continue to sell briskly at the Tower Records in Tokyo's Shibuya district, it's unlikely the Britishers who went Top 10 with "Breakout" will be autographing CDs at the Sam Goody in The Mall of America anytime soon.

#31

"King of Wishful Thinking" by Go West, 1990

And I'll tell myself I'm over you
'Cause I'm the king of wishful thinking

Peaked nationally at #8
Lead singer: Peter Cox
Written by Peter Cox, Richard Drummie, and Martin Page

In terms of all-time domestic box office receipts, *Pretty Woman* is ranked 60th, sandwiched between *Indiana Jones and the Temple of Doom* and *Tootsie*. The on-screen chemistry in that film between Julia Roberts and Richard Gere was outstanding, as was the soundtrack, which showcased music by Natalie Cole, David Bowie, Roy Orbison, and The Red Hot Chili Peppers, but it was Go West, the duo of Peter Cox and Richard Drummie, that really stole the show with their Top 10 smash "King of Wishful Thinking."

In the best vocal tradition of Bill Medley, Michael McDonald, and Dan Hartman, Peter Cox infuses Go West's hit with a poppy brand of blue-eyed soul that manages to be simultaneously smooth and gritty. "King of Wishful Thinking" would fit in beautifully on a compilation CD mixed among "(I've Had) The Time of My Life," "What a Fool Believes," and "I Can Dream About You."

It's interesting to note that a guy named Martin Page shares a writing credit on this record, as Page himself is a one-hit wonder, having scored a #14 single with his "In the House of Stone and Light" in 1995. This talented Britisher also co-penned Heart's "These Dreams," a coolly evocative Top 40 tune from the mid-80s. In addition, Page co-wrote "We Built This City," which San Francisco's Starship rocketed to #1.

For a track that is so strongly associated with *Pretty Woman*, it comes as no surprise that "King of Wishful Thinking" appears on albums like 1994's *Today's Movie Hits, Vol. 1*, as well as *Hollywood Movie Hits, Vol. 2*. On the latter collection, however, the song is covered by the Starlite Singers, an *ad hoc* outfit composed of anonymous session players. "King of Wishful Thinking" is also found on no fewer than four Go West compact discs: *Indian Summer, Aces and Kings: The Best of Go West, The Best of Go West,* and *The Greatest Hits*. By the way, nobody could be faulted for thinking that the last three titles sound curiously like they might very well be the exact same CD, but rest assured they are, in fact, three separate releases. Proof once more that a record company always walks a fine line between *marketing* its product and *milking* it.

While largely forgotten in the United States, Messrs. Cox and Drummie continue an active touring schedule in their native England, performing at outdoor music festivals and clubs throughout Britain, occasionally sharing the bill with Nick Heyward, the former lead singer of Haircut One Hundred. Close followers of New Wave will recall Haircut One Hundred as the one-hit wonders behind the #37 single "Love Plus One" from the summer of '82.

Finally, in 1987, Prince Charles staged a benefit called The Prince's Trust Rock Gala that featured artists such as Paul "Everytime You Go Away" Young, Alison Moyet, Bryan Adams, and Go West, who performed a tune called "Don't Look Down."

Brent's Two Cents: Members of the Go West fan club can be forgiven if they feel a touch ambivalent about their favorite group being included in *99 Red Balloons*. I mean, on the one hand, they're probably delighted that their boys are being written about, getting some positive ink, yet, on the other hand, they'd want readers to know that Go West actually charted three times, so they really aren't one-hit wonders at all.

Granted, in addition to "King of Wishful Thinking," Peter Cox and Richard Drummie also landed "Don't Look Down—The Sequel," as well as "Faithful" in the Top 40. As for the former, it spent a mere two weeks on the charts, peaking—peaking!—at #39, so I believe we can all agree that this song hardly qualifies as a bona fide hit. With respect to "Faithful," well, that's a little trickier. Yes, the tune topped out at a respectable #14 (although it was only #47 in sales) in early 1993, but 10 years later, unlike "King of Wishful Thinking," "Faithful" has vanished from the pop culture radar. You never hear this song on the radio anymore, and it's certainly not associated with any Hollywood blockbusters. Bottom line: Go West *is* a one-hit wonder.

#30

"I Can't Wait" by Nu Shooz, 1986

My love, tell me what it's all about
You've got something that I can't live without

Peaked nationally at #3
Lead singer: Valerie Day
Written by John Smith

The best urban dance records come out of places like Miami, New York, Detroit, Philadelphia, and Los Angeles, but what about Portland, Oregon? Well, the city famous for basketball's Trail Blazers, overcast skies, and bike paths spawned one of the most danceable hits in chart history in the form of "I Can't Wait" by Nu Shooz.

The group Nu Shooz, formed in 1979, was essentially the tandem of Valerie Day and John Smith, a married couple. Between 1982 and 1987, Nu Shooz issued three albums: *Can't Turn It Off, Poolside,* and *Told U So.* "I Can't Wait" appeared on *Poolside.*

What makes "I Can't Wait" such a classic one-hitter is the way it deftly blends elements of rock, disco, funk, and even electronica into a single, cohesive package. It's interesting to note that a good year before landing as a #3 radio smash, this Nu Shooz song had known tremendous success in discos worldwide. As was often the case during the 80s, the tastes of November's clubgoing hipsters in Manhattan and Berlin were having a huge hand in determining what teens in Orlando and Omaha would be hearing on their FM dials come July.

The most remarkable thing about "I Can't Wait" is the sheer number of compilation CDs on which it's been included: *Dance Mix USA Classics, Disco Queens: The 80's, Classic D.J. Mix, Volume 1, 80's: Hot Dance Trax, 18 Dance Mix Classics,* and *Freestyle Explosion, Vol. 1,* and there are at least a dozen more. If there was ever a tune meant to be a fun, worthy addition to any 80s collection, it's "I Can't Wait."

Nu Shooz, as mentioned before, called Portland home, as did an outfit dubbed Quarterflash, whom pop lovers will undoubtedly recall for their saxophone-fueled Top 5 charter "Harden My Heart" from 1981. Indeed, Nu Shooz and Quarterflash shared an eerily similar career trajectory: a meteoric rise on the strength of a smash 80s hit, then a quick fade. Incidentally, The Kingsmen ("Louie Louie"), Paul Revere and the Raiders ("Kicks"), Everclear ("I Will Buy You a New Life"), and Meredith Brooks ("Bitch") all hailed from Oregon.

Finally, and this can certainly be filed under "deep trivia," in April of 1986, as Nu Shooz was charting with "I Can't Wait," Stevie Nicks was also scoring with her own record called "I Can't Wait," which peaked at #16. It was an extremely rare instance of different songs with the exact same title holding down Top 40 spots concurrently.

Brent's Two Cents: At the height of their popularity, Nu Shooz did turns on TV shows like *Solid Gold* and *American Bandstand.* In fact, they even followed up "I Can't Wait," which I adore and count among my all-time favorite 80s singles, with the #28 "Point of No Return." Hoping to discover a forgotten pop gem, I downloaded "Point of No Return" off the Internet and gave it a listen. Well, er, how can I put this tactfully? The record goes absolutely nowhere. It's four and a half minutes of synthesizer and drum machine noodling, repetitive vocals, and zero hooks. What a disappointment, especially after such a promising debut with "I Can't Wait."

So, please, even though the talented Valerie Day and John Smith charted twice, let's not for a second categorize Nu Shooz as anything but a highly memorable one-hit wonder.

#29

"Lotta Love" by Nicolette Larson, 1978

My heart needs protection and so do I

Peaked nationally at #8
Lead singer: Nicolette Larson
Written by Neil Young

Yes, Neil Young wrote "Lotta Love." And, sure, The Jerry Garcia Band recorded an excellent cover of the tune. However, it was the late Nicolette Larson who really put the song on the pop map with her Top 10 smash back in 1978. Starting with its signature brassy introduction, "Lotta Love" smokes and grooves for a solid three minutes. Larson's strong, clear voice cuts through the track with equal measures of heartbreak and hope.

The pretty, diminutive Larson, who died in December of 1997 of a cerebral edema, packed a ton of music into her 45 years. The list of artists she worked with reads like a Who's Who of 70s and 80s pop/rock and country: Hoyt Axton, Christopher Cross, The Doobie Brothers, Linda Ronstadt, Commander Cody & His Lost Planet Airmen, Willie Nelson, The Beach Boys, and Emmylou Harris, to name just a few. By the way, Commander Cody might be recalled by one-hit fans for his "Hot Rod Lincoln," which cruised to #9 in 1972.

Although Nicolette Larson's overall career must absolutely be viewed as an unqualified success, it's still surprising that she charted only once. Granted, she did team up with Michael McDonald in 1980 for "Let Me Go, Love," a #35 single; however, her solo chart success began and ended with "Lotta Love." Like fellow one-hit wonders Karla Bonoff and The Sanford/Townsend Band, the argument can be made that in terms of racking up multiple radio hits, Larson broke onto the Top 40 scene at the wrong time. From a purely commercial standpoint, her sound would have been better suited to the airwaves of, say, 1972 through 1975, as opposed to the 1978-through-1980 period.

In the early 1980s, when it became apparent that Larson's pop albums would never approach Ronstadtian heights saleswise, the singer veered off in the direction of country. In fact, the Academy of Country Music voted her their Best New Vocalist of 1984. The apex, though, of Larson's foray into the country genre came in '86 when she recorded "That's How You Know When Love's Right," a smash duet with Steve Wariner. Incidentally, the 80s also saw Larson make her silver screen debut in the Danny DeVito and Arnold Schwarzenegger movie *Twins*. Predictably, she played the role of a nightclub songstress.

In February of 1998, just two months after her death, performers such as Jackson Browne, Bonnie Raitt, Jimmy Buffett, Carole King, and Crosby, Stills & Nash staged two concerts at Santa Monica's Civic Auditorium to honor their friend Nicolette Larson. The shows, poignantly called "It's Gonna Take a Lot of Love," raised several hundred thousand dollars for cancer research.

Insuring that Nicolette Larson lives on, "Lotta Love" is showcased on numerous CD collections: *Listen to the Music: '70s California Sound, Love Rocks, Vol. 5: After Midnight, No Nukes* (a live version pairing Larson with The Doobie Brothers), *Singers & Songwriters: 1978–1979*, and *The No. 1 Classic Pop Album*. This last compilation, *The No. 1 Classic Pop Album*, deserves special mention because, in addition to Larson, it features no fewer than four one-hit wonders: M ("Pop Muzik"), Norman Greenbaum ("Spirit in the Sky"), Amii Stewart ("Knock on Wood"), and Carl Douglas ("Kung Fu Fighting").

Finally, in 1995, Maureen McCormick, best known for her turn as

Marcia Brady on *The Brady Bunch*, issued *When You Get a Little Lonely* on the Phantom Hill label. This album's title cut was co-written by Nicolette Larson.

#28

"Cantaloop (Flip Fantasia)" by Us3, 1994

Feel the vibe from here to Asia
Dip, trip, flip fantasia

Peaked nationally at #9
Lead singer: Kobie Powell, Tukka Yoot, and Rahsaan Kelly
Written by Herbie Hancock, Rahsaan Kelly, Mel Simpson,
        and Geoff Wilkinson

Herbie Hancock's jazz classic "Cantaloupe Island" provided the backbone for this refreshing Top 10 record from 1994. However, it was precisely because of this jazzy influence that Us3 was destined to be a one-hit wonder.

The Top 40, needless to say, has shown little interest in jazz artists over the years. Granted, during the pre-Beatles/JFK era, someone like Dave Brubeck could dent the charts with his "Take Five" (#25 in 1961) or the Vince Guaraldi Trio might manage to score a modest #22 single with their "Cast Your Fate to the Wind" in 1963, but those were the rare exceptions. The pop charts have also occasionally welcomed tracks like "Morning Dance" by Spyro Gyra (#24 in 1979) or "Time and Tide" by Basia (#26 in 1988). However, this brand of "jazz-lite" has left no lasting mark. So, realizing the American mainstream's utter indifference to, if not outright disdain for, jazz, it was nothing short of amazing when Us3, a band of unknowns from London, rocketed "Cantaloop" to #9.

Us3's lone hit employed an unusual formula: rapping over jazz. It worked beautifully, and the track certainly stood apart from the other members of the Class of '94. FM listeners weren't confusing "Cantaloop" with "Stay (I Missed You)" by Lisa Loeb & Nine Stories or The Cranberries' "Linger," that's for sure.

The year 1993 saw Us3 release *Hand on the Torch*, their debut album, which spawned "Cantaloop (Flip Fantasia)." To this day, *Hand on the Torch* remains Blue Note Records' best-selling LP of all time. *Broadway & 52nd*, the outfit's 1997 sophomore effort, came and went with little fanfare. Of note, though, was the CD's title, Broadway and West 52nd Street in Manhattan being the first location of the legendary Birdland jazz club. In 1995, Us3 issued *She's the Word*, followed by 2001's *An Ordinary Day in an Unusual Place*, neither of which generated any chart action.

For such a hip, memorable song, it's surprising that "Cantaloop" was featured in two of Hollywood's more forgettable movies: *Super Mario Bros.*, the Bob Hoskins–John Leguizamo flick, as well as *It Takes Two*, the Mary-Kate and Ashley Olsen vehicle from 1995. As for compilations, Us3's smash is showcased on close to 30 compact disc collections, including *Living in the 90s*, where it shares the bill with

To date, Peter Frampton has released more than 34 full-length solo albums, yet he'll be forever remembered for just one: *Frampton Comes Alive!*, his gazillion-selling monster from 1976. So, you might call Peter Frampton the quintessential one-*album* wonder. Or, how about Britain's Fine Young Cannibals—four compact discs to their credit, but only *The Raw & the Cooked* is remembered today, as it spawned three hit singles: "She Drives Me Crazy," "Good Thing," and "Don't Look Back," the first two of which went all the way to #1. And, you could also add Julian Lennon to this one-album wonder list, as John's son is only remembered for 1984's *Valotte*.

one-hitters Right Said Fred ("I'm Too Sexy") and The Proclaimers ("I'm Gonna Be [500 Miles]"); *Hip Hop Jazz: Acid Metropolis, Vol.1; Dance Hits '94;* and *36 Hits: 1990–1994*, which also features "Wiggle It" by the rather obscure early 90s one-hit wonders 2 in a Room. "Cantaloop (Flip Fantasia)" also appeared on the soundtrack to the TV show *Beverly Hills 90210: The College Years*, in addition to being heard in 1994's *Renaissance Man*, a film that starred Danny DeVito and Mark Wahlberg.

#27

"Take on Me" by a-ha, 1985

Say it after me
It's no better to be safe than sorry

Peaked nationally at #1
Lead singer: Morten Harket
Written by Magne Furuholmen, Morten Harket, and Pal
        Waaktaar

a-ha's position on America's pop culture radar screen is both fasci- nating and curious. On the one hand, when VH-1 named their 100 Greatest Videos of All Time, the band's smash "Take on Me" landed at #8. MTV, for their part, ranked "Take on Me" as the 14th best video ever. In fact, it's no exaggeration to call this song a genuine 80s touchstone, a musical icon of the MTV Generation. However, all that being said, you'd be hard pressed to come up with a friend, family member, or co-worker who could name even a single member of this New Wave trio from Norway. (Hint: Magne Furuholmen, Morten Harket, and Pal Waaktaar.) By the same token, you could approach, say, four or five complete strangers on a New York City subway platform, and it's entirely possible at least one of them could, right there on the spot, launch into an elaborately detailed description of a-ha's nearly 20-year-old video. "Oh, I remember that one! It was totally cool because it mixed animation with, you know, real life—it's a technique called 'rotoscope,' or something like that. Anyway, this young blonde girl's in a diner having a cup of coffee, reading a comic book, when all of a sudden this hand reaches right up out of the page and pulls her *into* the comic book itself. Next thing you know, she's running frantically with this handsome dude as they're being chased by two evil motorcyclists, one of whom is wielding a wrench. . . ." Ask that same person to name the *album* "Take on Me" first appeared on—a blank stare and silence. (Answer: *Hunting High and Low.*) Again, it's remarkable, indeed paradoxical, that in some ways we can know so much about a one-hit wonder, yet at the same time know virtually nothing about them.

"Take on Me" went all the way to #1 in nine different countries, including the United States and Germany. Interestingly, though, when the record was first released in the U.K. in '84, fewer than 300 copies of the 45 were sold. Hardly an auspicious debut for an outfit that has now sold more than 30 million albums worldwide. But, after a-ha retooled the track, mainly adding more synthesizer, "Take on Me" positively tore up the charts. By the way, movie fans might recall a-ha's hit from *Corky Romano*, the Chris Kattan flick. Also, Reel Big Fish, the ska-punksters, contributed a manic "Take on Me" cover to the *BASEketball* soundtrack. a-ha's other silver screen moment occurred in 1987 when they recorded the title song to the James Bond film *The Living Daylights*, which featured Timothy Dalton as 007.

Almost a quarter-century after forming, a-ha continues releasing albums, 2002's *Lifelines* being their latest offering. The group also maintains an active touring schedule, performing primarily in Europe and Japan.

Brent's Two Cents: Of all 101 one-hitters on our survey, a-ha was by far the most difficult to establish a ranking for. The band ultimately checked in at a very respectable #27, but, quite frankly, had *99 Red*

Balloons' final order been determined on, say, a Thursday rather than a Wednesday, the Norwegians easily could have scored in the Top 5. I mean, I personally think every artist showcased in this book is terrific in their own way, so it's somewhat silly for me to state, for example, that The First Class and their "Beach Baby" at #4 is 23 positions *better* than a-ha and "Take on Me." I can, however, say without hesitation that if sheer *memorability* was the sole criterion in rating a one-hit wonder, a strong argument could be made for putting a-ha at #1, based on the indisputable fact that if you were anywhere near a radio or television in the mid-80s, to this day, you retain vivid memories of "Take on Me."

#26

"I'm Gonna Be (500 Miles)" by The Proclaimers, 1993

But I would walk 500 miles
And I would walk 500 more

Peaked nationally at #3
Lead singers: Charlie Reid and Craig Reid
Written by Charlie Reid and Craig Reid

The Proclaimers are brothers Charlie and Craig Reid, Scotland's most famous twins. They hail from Edinburgh, the same city that spawned the Bay City Rollers. It's no exaggeration to say that Messrs. Reid and Reid would be *no*-hit wonders, at least in America, if not for the actress Mary Stuart Masterson and a largely overlooked movie from the early 90s called *Benny & Joon*, which starred Masterson, Aidan Quinn, and Johnny Depp. Hollywood legend holds that Masterson was a tremendous fan of *Sunshine on Leith*, a Proclaimers' album virtually unknown in the States, and the actress's particular enthusiasm for the CD's first track, "I'm Gonna Be (500 Miles)," was such that she persuaded the film's director Jeremiah Chechik to include it in the picture. *Benny & Joon* opened on hundreds of screens from Seattle to Cincinnati and soon "I'm Gonna Be" was all over the radio. Speaking of movies, The Proclaimers can also be heard on the *Shrek* soundtrack, doing a number called "I'm on My Way," as well as in *Dumb & Dumber*, with a cover of the Motown classic "Get Ready."

What makes The Proclaimers' lone hit so memorable is its unabashed Scottishness. To hear Charlie and Craig Reid sing is to be instantly transported to the verdant land of haggis, Hogmanay, and hangovers via a few too many McEwan's Exports. Indeed, the lads' singing voices make Scrooge McDuck, he of the stereotypical, over-the-top cartoon brogue, seem like a carpetbagger. So thick are The Proclaimers' accents that they actually poked fun at the very fact in their tune called "Throw the 'R' Away." By the way, "I'm Gonna Be (500 Miles)" might be the only Top 40 record to ever include the word "haver," although it comes out sounding like "heaver" to a Yank's ear. To "haver" simply means to babble or talk nonsense.

Interestingly, "I'm Gonna Be" was part of a compact disc compilation called *1988: 20 Original Chart Hits*, yet the song also appears on *Billboard Top Hits: 1993*. The former collection, which was issued in 1997, is actually guilty of a bit of revisionist history in that, yes, the

Like The Proclaimers, a singer named Ali Thomson hails from Scotland. Thomson scored a #15 single with "Take a Little Rhythm" back in the summer of 1980. It was his only taste of the Top 40. And, eight years before "Take a Little Rhythm" charted, an outfit called the Royal Scots Dragoon Guards, obviously also from the home of Sean Connery, Sheena Easton, and The Simple Minds, earned one-hitter status when their "Amazing Grace" instrumental soared all the way to #11.

single was originally released in the late 80s, but it didn't even get a sniff of the U.S. charts until *Benny & Joon* was screened five years later. Kudos to *1988: 20 Original Chart Hits* for correctly identifying "I'm Gonna Be" as vintage '88, but to call it a *hit* from that year is not accurate.

Incidentally, in a 2002 episode of *The Simpsons*, where Homer Simpson installs a satellite TV dish, he can be heard singing gleefully about the prospect of having "500 channels" to the tune of "I'm Gonna Be (500 Miles)."

Today, The Proclaimers continue making records and playing live gigs, both in Europe and here in the States. Venues such as The Fillmore in San Francisco, West Hollywood's Troubador, Chicago's House of Blues, and B.B. King's Blues Club in Manhattan have all hosted the Brothers Reid in recent years.

#25

"Dancing in the Moonlight" by King Harvest, 1973

It's such a fine and natural sight
Everybody's dancing in the moonlight

Peaked nationally at #13
Lead singer: Ron Altbach
Written by Sherman Kelly

What makes King Harvest's lone hit record so memorable is the way its bright, tinkling electric piano riff plays against a deep, chunky bass line, especially during the song's instantly recognizable introduction.

"Dancing in the Moonlight," a let-your-hair-down-and-boogie track from the early 70s, spent nearly three months in the Top 40. Other one-hitters sharing the charts around the same time as King Harvest's radio run included Vicki "The Night the Lights Went Out in Georgia" Lawrence and Chi Coltrane, the pretty Wisconsin-born singer who scored a #17 single with "Thunder and Lightning."

King Harvest, who operated out of New York City, released only two albums: *Dancing in the Moonlight*, which obviously yielded their famous single, followed by 1976's highly forgettable LP simply called *King Harvest*. The main reason the band failed to achieve greater commercial success, and is recalled today as a one-hit wonder, rested on the fact that much of their material displayed a definite country, bluesy flavor, somewhat reminiscent of The Grateful Dead. An interesting sound to be sure; however, certainly not one that would have made your group a radio staple back in the 70s. A kid plunking down his $3.50 to see King Harvest perform live in concert during the summer of '73 would have been extremely disappointed if he expected a 10-song set of AM solid gold.

Before forming King Harvest, several members of the band were part of a group strangely named Buffalongo. This outfit waxed their own version of "Dancing in the Moonlight," a track containing a rolling, bluesy organ. The Buffalongo boys got down and dirty, putting, as Ike Turner might have said, some *real stink* into that "Moonlight." However, it's a little-known fact, even among pop historians, that the obscure English duo of Jason Crest and Brian Bennett, billing themselves as High Broom, recorded "Dancing in the Moonlight" before either King Harvest or Buffalongo. High Broom's effort was released as a 45 on the Island label in 1970, the B-side of which was the tune "Percy's on the Run."

Fans of Liza Minnelli will probably recall her 1973 LP *Liza Minnelli, The Singer*. But how many will remember that Ms. Liza paid serious homage to the one-hit wonder on that album? She included "Dancing in the Moonlight," as well as "Oh, Babe, What Would You Say?" made famous by the classic one-hitter Hurricane Smith.

Apart from King Harvest's, the best take on "Dancing in the Moonlight" was provided by Toploader, five lads from Eastbourne, England. While Toploader enjoyed tremendous success in 2000 with this single in their native U.K., the track never dented the Top 40 in America.

By the way, Ron Altbach, the guy who sang lead on "Dancing in the Moonlight," penned a few tunes for The Beach Boys. If you ever listen to the Boys' rather forgettable LP *M.I.U. Album* from 1978, you'll hear Altbach's "Belles of Paris" and "She's Got Rhythm."

Brent's Two Cents: Remember those "Do you know me?" American Express TV spots from the 70s? King Harvest would have been ideal candidates for a rock 'n' roll version of that ad campaign: "Do you know us? We scored a Top 20 smash that was all over the radio in '73—in fact, for a couple of months, you couldn't get away from our song. Yet, whenever we go out on the streets of Manhattan, nobody recognizes us."

I always envisioned King Harvest as being four well-dressed black guys from Detroit, such was the soulful, urban vibe of "Dancing in the Moonlight." Imagine my surprise when I saw the band's picture for the first time: a half-dozen scruffy, bearded white dudes who looked like they'd just arrived in town from a year in a backwoods cabin.

Incidentally, "Dancing in the Moonlight" was prominently featured in the Alec Baldwin movie *Outside Providence*, indisputably one of the biggest dogs of 1999.

#24

"Someday, Someway" by Marshall Crenshaw, 1982

Someday, someway
Maybe I'll understand you

Peaked nationally at #36
Lead singer: Marshall Crenshaw
Written by Marshall Crenshaw

"Jangly, black-coffee-with-five-sugars pop" best described "Someday, Someway," as Marshall Crenshaw suffused his lone Top 40 hit with a gleeful, manic energy reminiscent of early Beatles tracks like "All My Loving" and "Can't Buy Me Love." In a year that introduced (some would say "subjected") radio listeners to Buckner & Garcia's "Pac-Man Fever," as well as Charlene and her "I've Never Been to Me," Crenshaw's well-crafted single went a long way toward rescuing the one-hit wonder Class of '82 from complete embarrassment.

Fans of Michael Keaton will remember "Someday, Someway" from the *Night Shift* soundtrack. Crenshaw also contributed music to *Superman III*, another early 80s flick. Speaking of movies, the singer acted in a couple himself, playing the role of Buddy Holly in 1987's *La Bamba*, which told the story of rock 'n' roll legend Richie Valens; while also appearing a year earlier as a musician in *Peggy Sue Got Married*, the Francis Ford Coppola film starring Kathleen Turner and Nicolas Cage. His first professional acting experience, however, came in the late 70s when he portrayed John Lennon in the West Coast touring production of the Broadway show *Beatlemania*. More than most of his musical contemporaries, Crenshaw has often expressed, through interviews and writings, a deep appreciation for the pioneering rockers of the late 50s and early 60s, citing their tremendous influence on his own music. So it's hardly a surprise that he's made a conscious effort throughout his career to get involved with projects that have a strong connection to the likes of Holly, Valens, and The Fab Four.

For a tune that hardly set the airwaves on fire, reaching only as high as #36 and spending just a month on the charts, "Someday, Someway" has displayed incredible staying power. A taste of the Crenshaw track was heard in 2000 on the NBC show *Ed*, while the WB's *Roswell* featured it in a 2001 episode. The cut was also showcased in *Mr. Deeds*, the Adam Sandler film, although, curiously, it wasn't part of the accompanying soundtrack issued on compact disc. Two decades after its release, the song is still very much a presence on the cultural radar.

"Someday, Someway" was originally taken off the Detroit native's debut album, the eponymous *Marshall Crenshaw*. In recent years, it's found its way onto several compilation CDs as well, including *18 New Wave Classics, Volume 2* from 1997, which also highlighted the notable one-hitters 'til tuesday ("Voices Carry"), a-ha ("Take on Me"), and Frank Zappa ("Valley Girl"). (Yes, "Valley Girl" was the only Top 40 single for the late, great leader of The Mothers of Invention. Frank Zappa and Marshall Crenshaw: More proof that you can be famous, talented, and well respected and *still* go down in pop/rock annals as a one-hit wonder.) In addition, "Someday, Someway" is on *Just Can't Get Enough: New Wave Hits of the 80's, Vol. 5*, where it shares space with "867-5309/Jenny" by one-hitter Tommy Tutone.

Interestingly, Crenshaw enjoyed his greatest chart success back in the mid-90s when a song he co-wrote, "Til I Hear It from You," zoomed all the way to #11 for The Gin Blossoms, spending an astonishing 33 weeks in the Top 40. Movie buffs will recall "Til I Hear It from You" from *Empire Records,* a quirky sleeper from 1995 starring Liv Tyler and Renée Zellweger.

Today, Marshall Crenshaw continues making albums—15 and counting at last tally. He also maintains an active schedule of club dates at venues like The Bottom Line in New York City, Schubas Tavern in Chicago, and Hollywood's Knitting Factory.

#23

"Have I the Right?"
by The Honeycombs, 1964

Have I the right to kiss you?
You know I'll always miss you

Peaked nationally at #5
Lead singer: Denis D'Ell
Written by Howard Blaikley

The Honeycombs featured a rarity among rock groups: a female drummer by the name of Ann "Honey" Lantree. Denis D'Ell, John Lantree, Martin Murray, and Alan Ward rounded out the band, which, incidentally, was originally dubbed The Sherabons.

In terms of timing, The Honeycombs' could not have been worse. Just as the group was making its mark in the Top 40 with "Have I the Right?," The Beatles were gathering a full head of steam, muscling competing acts right off the charts. What's more, as their single was steadily climbing both the American and British charts, The Honeycombs found themselves on the other side of the world in Australia in the midst of an extensive tour. In hindsight, they should have been back home in London, or in New York on *The Ed Sullivan Show*, launching a follow-up. Incidentally, besides "Have I the Right?," the only other Honeycombs tune to make any noise was "I Can't Stop," which topped out at #48.

"Have I the Right?" has often been called a toe-tapper. Well, the term "toe-tapper" doesn't even begin to capture the high energy displayed in this incredibly bouncy record. "Foot-stomper" or "table-banger" would be a more apt description. Indeed, "Glad All Over" and "Bits and Pieces" done by fellow Londoners The Dave Clark Five are perhaps the only other tunes from that era to even approach the manic, beat flavor of "Have I the Right?"

The Honeycombs' lone hit appeared on their self-titled debut album *The Honeycombs*; however, "Have I the Right?" has, over the years, surfaced on more than two dozen other LPs, including compilations like the groovily named *Cappuccino Classics, Vol. 3: Girls Girls Girls*, where it followed "Happy Together" by The Turtles. The song was also showcased on *Bubble Rock Is Here to Stay*, even though "Have I the Right?" could hardly be classified as bubblegum.

No discussion of The Honeycombs is complete without a nod to a fellow named Joe Meek, the man who produced the band, and who is actually considered by students of early 60s Britpop to be more integral to The Honeycombs' success than the actual members themselves, primarily because he was responsible for shaping the group's distinctive sound with his post-production wizardry. Time compression, reverb, distortion, and tons of echo were hallmarks of a Meek-produced single, and they were all in evidence on "Have I the Right?"

To this day, Meek, who took his own life in 1967 at the age of 37, remains a cult figure in the U.K., partly due to his involvement with outfits like The Honeycombs and partly on the strength of an instrumental piece he wrote more than 40 years ago called "Telstar," which The Tornadoes drove all the way to #1 in 1962. In fact, The Tornadoes, who were essentially a studio outfit organized by Meek, hold the honor of being the first English act to ever land the top position on the American pop charts, beating even the likes of The Beatles and The Rolling Stones to the punch. Incidentally, records such as "Telstar," Al Hirt's "Java," and "Classical Gas" by one-hitter Mason Williams were the kind of instrumental hits from the 60s that disk jockeys on middle-of-the-road AM stations like WBZ in Boston and KNBR in San Francisco relied on well into the 1970s when they needed to fill a minute or less of airtime as they "headed for news at the top of the hour. . . ."

Joe Meek's death spelled an abrupt end for The Honeycombs, as the group disbanded in 1967 after a four-year run. In 2002, however, EMI issued *Have I the Right: The Very Best of The Honeycombs*, making one of the brightest, snappiest sounds in pop history available on compact disc.

#22

"Right Here, Right Now" by Jesus Jones, 1991

*Right here, right now, there is no other place I want
    to be
Right here, right now, watching the world wake up
    from history*

Peaked nationally at #2
Lead singer: Mike Edwards
Written by Mike Edwards

"Right Here, Right Now" was the chart smash from the album *Doubt*, Jesus Jones's sophomore release following 1989's barely noticed *Liquidizer*. The radio version of this tune ran an economical, no-nonsense two minutes and thirty-two seconds, making "Right Here, Right Now" the sort of hit record listeners were eager to hear played again and again. This short song just plain wore well over the course of its 15-week Top 40 run.

The thick, driving bass line really stood out on this single, especially during the track's let's-get-down-to-business introduction. Indeed, "Right Here, Right Now's" 19-second opening was among the catchiest, most memorable riffs from the entire decade of the 90s, as it seemed to come out of nowhere and establish an immediate groove.

On October 8, 1991, Jesus Jones performed "Right Here, Right Now" on *The Tonight Show*. Jay Leno's other guests that evening were James Earl Jones, John "Insert-Your-Own-Joke-Here" Tesh, and the actress Roma Downey. That year also saw the Londoners take home an MTV award for Best New Artist in a Video. Incidentally, one-hitters 'til tuesday and a-ha had captured the same honor from MTV in '85 and '86, respectively. With massive television and radio exposure, why

Is nothing sacred? Well, apparently not, at least when it comes to naming bands. In addition to Jesus Jones, we've known Northern Ireland's Moses K & the Prophets, a mysterious outfit formed back in the mid 60s; Buddha on the Moon from Houston; God Street Wine, the jam band that got its start in Manhattan in the late 1980s; The Jesus & Mary Chain of Glasgow, Scotland; the metal-heads called God & Texas; The Buddha Blessed; Jehovah's Waitresses from Ottawa, Ontario; Brahma; and, of course, the Mahavishnu Orchestra, the jazzy rockers who enjoyed a wide following in the 70s.

wasn't Jesus Jones able to build on the success of "Right Here, Right Now" and become staples of the FM airwaves? That question can be answered in four simple words: too British, too techno. By the early 90s, mainstream pop tastes were leaning heavily in the direction of artists like Mariah Carey, Janet Jackson, Vanessa Williams, and Whitney Houston. These unmistakably American singers left little room on the charts for an outfit like Jesus Jones, whose sound, in many ways, would have fit in better with the English New Wavers of the early 80s such as Naked Eyes, Thompson Twins, and Eurythmics.

"Right Here, Right Now" appears on several compilation CDs, most notably *Living in the '90s*, put out on the Razor & Tie label. In addition to Jesus Jones, this collection includes classic one-hit wonders The Proclaimers ("I'm Gonna Be [500 Miles]"), House of Pain ("Jump Around"), R*S*F ("I'm Too Sexy"), and Us3 ("Cantaloop [Flip Fantasia]"). Interestingly, NBC briefly employed "Right Here, Right Now" to promote its *Nightly News* program, the network brass apparently feeling the tune embodied the *zeitgeist* circa 1991, with specific reference to the fall of Communism in Eastern Europe.

Lastly, the very early 90s must inarguably go down as one of the best eras in one-hit wonder history, featuring Deee-Lite and their "Groove Is in the Heart" from 1990, "I Touch Myself" by Divinyls,

Oleta Adams's "Get Here," "Walking in Memphis" by Marc Cohn, and of course, Jesus Jones's "Right Here, Right Now," all from the golden year 1991.

#21

"Keep Your Hands to Yourself" by The Georgia Satellites, 1986

My honey, my baby, don't put my love on no shelf
She said, "Don't hand me no lines and keep your
hands to yourself!"

Peaked nationally at #2
Lead singer: Dan Baird
Written by Dan Baird

The Georgia Satellites' "Keep Your Hands to Yourself" charted in 1986; however, this record would have been equally at home in 1956, 1966, 1976, or even 1996, as it's just a timeless, kick-out-the-jambs rock 'n' roll number.

Dan Baird digs into the song's vocals with a no-holds-barred zest straight out of a rowdy Texas honky-tonk. In fact, for some inexplicable reason, '86 yielded an inordinate number of Top 40 tunes that plain rocked: "Walk of Life" by Dire Straits, Simple Minds' "Alive and Kicking," "Sledgehammer" by Peter Gabriel, and Stevie Nicks's "Talk to Me." That same year also produced a bounty of smooth, well-crafted singles like "The Sweetest Taboo" by Sade, Mr. Mister's "Broken Wings" and "Kyrie," as well as "True Colors" by Cyndi Lauper and Bruce Hornsby and the Range's "The Way It Is." A strong case can be made for calling those 12 calendar months in the mid-80s pop's high-water mark in terms of variety and quality, better than any seen in the previous quarter-century. Whether you were a New Yorker listening to WNBC's last gasps on the AM dial or a San Franciscan tuned to a thriving KYUU-FM, 1986 provided consistently memorable music.

So, it was into this fertile chart soil that The Georgia Satellites found themselves planted, poised to flourish. Why, then, are these talented guys from Atlanta remembered for being quintessential one-hit wonders? Well, as strange as it sounds, the answer is simply that their lone hit was so distinctive it rendered a successful follow-up virtually impossible. "Keep Your Hands to Yourself," like, for example, "You Get What You Give" by New Radicals or Dexys Midnight Runners' "Come on Eileen," is one of those rare tracks that so masterfully embodies a group's musical essence, a second act would be superfluous. And, at the risk of sounding too Zen-like, certain bands are probably just destined to be classic one-hitters.

"Keep Your Hands to Yourself" originally appeared on the album

---

Are they or aren't they? Only their DJ knows for sure...

Should Lee Michaels be considered a one-hit wonder? In 1971, he drives "Do You Know What I Mean" to #6, a solid hit by any measure. However, his follow-up, "Can I Get a Witness," spends a solitary week in the Top 40, peaking at a just-barely-makes-it #39. Or how about the Big Bopper? Like Lee Michaels, he scores a #6 single with the 50s classic "Chantilly Lace," then charts for the only other time at #38 with "Big Bopper's Wedding." Finally, you be the jury in the case of Albert Hammond: He has a #5 smash in '72 with "It Never Rains in Southern California." The English-born singer follows that up with the totally forgotten "I'm a Train" at an anemic #31. So, is it fair to refer to Lee Michaels, the Big Bopper, and Albert Hammond as one-hitters? Well, as the announcer used to intone on those old IBM/NFL television spots: You make the call!

Georgia Satellites. In 1995, WEA/Rhino issued *18 Screamers from the 80's*, which showcased Sammy Hagar's "I Can't Drive 55," one-hit wonder Scandal's "The Warrior," in addition to The Georgia Satellites' #2 smash. "Keep Your Hands to Yourself" was also part of a compact disc called *ABC Monday Night Football: Official Party Album,* the only compilation to ever feature Jerry Reed's "When You're Hot, You're Hot," "Soul Man" by Sam & Dave, *and* Wang Chung's "Everybody Have Fun Tonight."

By the way, after leaving The Georgia Satellites, Dan Baird released *Love Songs for the Hearing Impaired* in the early 90s. The album spawned "I Love You Period," a song that peaked at #26. It was his first and only hit single, making Baird a *two-time* one-hitter, initially as frontman of a band, then as a solo act. Interestingly enough, Bryan Ferry accomplished this same feat when he joined his Roxy Music mates in charting at #30 with "Love Is the Drug" in 1976, followed a dozen years later with his own #31 track "Kiss and Tell."

#20

"More Today Than Yesterday" by The Spiral Starecase, 1969

I love you more today than yesterday
But only half as much as tomorrow

Peaked nationally at #12
Lead singer: Pat Upton
Written by Pat Upton

In the fall of 2002, K-EARTH 101, Los Angeles's powerhouse Oldies station, asked listeners to name their all-time favorite one-hit singles from the 60s. Here were the top responses: number three, "Time Won't Let Me" by The Outsiders; number two, "Girl Watcher" by The

O'Kaysions; and number one, "More Today Than Yesterday" by The Spiral Starecase.

If ever a one-hit wonder displayed genuine staying power, it would have to be this song. More than three decades after its release, The Spiral Starecase's lone Top 40 hit still surfaces regularly on the pop culture radar screen. Viewers of TV's *Ally McBeal* will remember an episode called "Silver Bells," where Greg Germann, who played the show's smarmy senior partner, Richard Fish, is heard singing "More Today Than Yesterday." Movie buffs might recall the original version appearing on the soundtracks of *My Girl* and *The Waterboy*.

"More Today Than Yesterday" rates as one of the greatest one-hit wonders of all time primarily on the strength of Pat Upton's crystalline lead vocal, which is energetic without being overpowering. Upton's clear tenor, combined with the effective use of a fat brass section, rendered The Spiral Starecase a sort of under-achieving, "if only . . . / what might have been" Chicago.

The group was composed of Harvey Kaye, Dick Lopes, Vinnie Parello, Bob Raymond, and Pat Upton. Interestingly, though, of the five Starecase members, only Upton is heard on the original recording of "More Today Than Yesterday," as the song was cut using studio musicians. In fact, *More Today Than Yesterday*, the outfit's eponymous debut album (indeed, their only album), was waxed *after* their tune became a hit as a 45 r.p.m. single.

Although you won't hear these versions on your local Oldies station, artists as diverse as Lena Horne, Patti Austin, and Danny Gans have all recorded the Pat Upton–penned classic. However, the most inventive take on this number, hands down, belongs to Charles Earland, a jazz organist who enjoys a small, but enthusiastic following. In 1970, just a year after The Spiral Starecase single dominated the AM airwaves, Earland, along with help from a young sax man named Grover Washington, Jr., recorded a live instrumental "More Today Than Yesterday" that positively cooks from start to finish.

And if you were wondering about the spelling, among pop and rock bands, no outfit ever had its name as consistently misspelled as

In addition to The Spiral Starecase, the late 60s spawned such memorable one-hit wonders as The Lemon Pipers ("Green Tambourine"), Paul Mauriat ("Love Is Blue"), Blue Cheer ("Summertime Blues"), Merrilee Rush & the Turnabouts ("Angel of the Morning"), Mason Williams ("Classical Gas"), The O'Kaysions ("Girl Watcher"), The Crazy World of Arthur Brown ("Fire"), and Flying Machine ("Smile a Little Smile for Me").

The Spiral Starecase—Dexys Midnight Runners included. The group reportedly took the name from *The Spiral Staircase*, a long-forgotten 1946 thriller starring Dorothy McGuire, George Brent, and Elsa Lanchester. Why Pat Upton and his Sacramento, California, mates chose the funky twist on the spelling remains a mystery. Incidentally, The Spiral Starecase were originally known as The Fydallions. Hey, it was the groovy 60s, after all.

#19

"Tubthumping" by Chumbawamba, 1997

I get knocked down, but I get up again
And you're never going to keep me down

Peaked nationally at #6
Lead singer: Dunstan Bruce
Written by Chumbawamba

Although this first track ["Tubthumping"] comes charging out of the gate, the album quickly takes a nose-dive

and falls flat on its face. The following cuts are nothing
like the first and simply do not measure up, which is disappointing. Save money, buy the single.
                    —ERIN O'BRIEN-KENNA, REVIEWING *TUBTHUMPER*,
                    THE ALBUM THAT SPAWNED "TUBTHUMPING," IN
                    AQUARIAN WEEKLY, OCTOBER 1, 1997

Starting in the fall of 1997, this gleefully rowdy tune embarked on an
amazing six-month race through the Top 40 charts, rocketing all the
way to #6. In the process, it introduced Chumbawamba to a huge
American audience that had, pre-"Tubthumping," been completely
unaware of its nearly 15-year existence on the other side of the
Atlantic. Although they never managed to score a second hit, Chumbawamba, hailing from Leeds, England, still remains to this day the only
self-proclaimed "anarchists" to ever enjoy heavy rotation on VH-1.

Dunstan Bruce is credited with the lead vocals on "Tubthumping,"
but with eccentrically named bandmate Alice Nutter chiming in with
her angelic "pissing the night aways," not to mention raucous soccer
chants throughout, it's really not fair or accurate to credit any one
person with carrying the main singing load on this record. Imagine
Petula Clark doing her mid-60s hit "Downtown" layered over the
sounds of a football stadium full of inebriated fans screaming at top

---

Did you see *Dirty Work*, a very funny movie from 1998
starring Norm Macdonald and Jack Warden?
"Tubthumping" was on the soundtrack. What about
Varsity Blues, another film from the late 90s, which fea-
tured Amy Smart and James Van Der Beek?
Chumbawamba's #6 smash could be heard in that flick, as
well. *Air Bud 2*, *Senseless*, and *Joe Somebody*—
"Tubthumping" also turned up in those three pictures.
British anarchists contributing music to mainstream
Hollywood movies—you gotta love it!

volume and you'll begin to get at the infectious energy and zaniness of "Tubthumping." Incidentally, the term "tubthumping" is British slang for what we in the States might call street-corner preaching. If you've ever visited Speaker's Corner in London's Hyde Park, you've undoubtedly witnessed some world-class tubthumping.

In addition to the aforementioned Alice Nutter, the group also boasts a Danbert Nobacon. The British do possess a certain goofy flair when it comes to names, don't they? Speaking of strange names, Chumbawamba claims their moniker came from a band member's dream wherein he saw two bathroom doors, one of which was marked Chumba, the other Wamba.

In 1986, Chumbawamba released their debut effort, an album called *Pictures of Starving Children Sell Records*, which has to be ranked among the most provocative LP titles of all time. Years later, in 1999, the band issued *Uneasy Listening* (another superb title), a "greatest hits" collection that included the "hits" "Mouthful of Shit," "On the Day the Nazi Died," as well as "Give the Anarchist a Cigarette."

And finally, Keith Flint, of the *no-hit* British electronica outfit The Prodigy, once gave an interview where he said how much he liked Chumbawamba, even if it did take them "fifteen years to write one fucking hit song." Ouch!

#18

"Get a Job" by The Silhouettes, 1958

Yip yip yip yip yip yip yip yip
Mum mum mum mum mum mum
Get a job! Sha na na na, sha na na na na

Peaked nationally at #1
Lead singer: Bill Horton
Written by Earl Beal, Raymond Edwards, Bill Horton, and
        Rick Lewis

The Drifters, The Coasters, The Jive Five, The Moonglows, The Platters, The Del-Vikings, The Orioles, The Paragons, The Skyliners, and of course, The Silhouettes—if you hoped to enjoy success as a doo-wop group back in the 50s and 60s, there apparently was an unwritten rule that you had to include the word "the" in your name.

The Silhouettes, who were originally dubbed The Thunderbirds, were composed of Earl Beal (baritone), Raymond Edwards (bass), Bill Horton (lead singer), and Rick Lewis (tenor). With the exception of Lewis, all of the guys had been members of an outfit with the colorful name of the Gospel Tornadoes.

It takes talent to write a hit single about, say, a broken heart or being madly in love; however, it takes a special genius to write a #1 song about *unemployment*, which is precisely what The Silhouettes did. "Get a Job" is an unforgettable one-hitter because of how effectively it touches on a universal theme. Nearly everybody can relate, at one time or another, to just how crummy it feels to be out of work, moping around the house, dejectedly poring over the Help Wanted ads.

Ironically, considering the glum subject matter, The Silhouettes imbued their record with a genuine sense of glee. Between the "sha na na nas," the "yip yip yips" and Ronnie McGill's energetic, punchy sax solo, "Get a Job" manages to create an upbeat, hopeful mood throughout: Sure, I may be unemployed, with my girlfriend on my case, but you know what? Somehow everything's going to be okay.

Considering that The Silhouettes hailed from Philadelphia, it's only appropriate that "Get a Job" can be found on a compilation called *Philly Favorites*, a CD issued in 1999 by Oldies station WOGL. Forgotten gems like "Expressway (To Your Heart)" by Soul Survivors and Harold Melvin & the Blue Notes' "Bad Luck" are also part of this collection. If you can't get your hands on *Philly Favorites*, look for "Get a Job" on *Double Date with Joanie and Chachi*, a compact disc released in the the late 90s by the campy Nick at Nite Records.

Of course, the doo-wop devotees among us would insist on tracking down The Silhouettes' lone chart hit on 45, where it was pressed on the Ember label. However, hardcore rock 'n' roll purists would take matters even a step beyond, scouring collectibles shops and Delaware Valley yard sales for the original 1957 release, which appeared on the obscure Junior Records label, before ultimately landing on Ember for national distribution. Incidentally, the flip side to "Get a Job" was a tune called "I Am Lonely." A 45 record featuring songs of *unemployment* and *loneliness*—well, certainly no one can accuse The Silhouettes of borrowing a pair of Pat Boone's late 50s rose-colored glasses.

Hollywood, by the way, has embraced "Get a Job" over the years, especially during the 70s and 80s, when it appeared on soundtracks for successful movies such as *American Graffiti*, *The Flamingo Kid*, and *Stand by Me*.

Sadly, only one of The Silhouettes, Rick Lewis, remains alive today, with Bill Horton, Raymond Edwards, and Earl Beal having passed away in 1995, 1997, and 2001, respectively.

#17

"Life in a Northern Town" by The Dream Academy, 1986

A Salvation Army band played
And the children drank lemonade

Peaked nationally at #7
Lead singer: Nick Laird-Clowes
Written by Nick Laird-Clowes and Gilbert Gabriel

This ["Life in a Northern Town"] was in the charts when I
was living in a northern town, aged 17, hating the rules
of my parents, hating the pettiness at school, wanting to
escape. It seemed that the recurrent theme of eighties
pop music was an angst-ridden desire to get out of
Dullsville, Northern Town.

—GERT, POSTED ON MADMUSINGSOF.ME.UK

"Tarzan Boy" by Baltimora, "The Captain of Her Heart" by Double,
"Shake You Down" by Gregory Abbott, and "Keep Your Hands to Yourself" by The Georgia Satellites—1985 and 1986 were fertile years for
one-hit wonders. However, no one-hitter from that period is more
memorable than The Dream Academy's "Life in a Northern Town," a
rare Top 10 smash that mentions The Beatles, Frank Sinatra, *and*
John F. Kennedy.

"Life in a Northern Town" was written as a tribute to Nick Drake,
the well-respected English singer and songwriter who died in 1974 at
the age of 26. Interestingly, in sort of a six-degrees-of-separation
connection, Drake had recorded with Doris "Just One Look" Troy, a
classic 1960s one-hitter who is featured on our tour at #97.

The Dream Academy was composed of Britishers Nick Laird-

Clowes, Kate St. John, and Gilbert Gabriel. St. John belonged to a group called The Ravishing Beauties before joining The Academy, while Laird-Clowes did prior stints with two long-forgotten outfits, Alfalfa and The Act.

In December of 1985, The Dream Academy performed "Life in a Northern Town" on *Saturday Night Live*. Actress Teri Garr hosted the show. Perhaps foreshadowing the trio's status as one-hit wonders, *SNL* booked a rare *second* musical guest that evening, The Cult, an 80s band out of Bradford, England. The Cult sang "She Sells Sanctuary" on the program.

Fans of *Ferris Bueller's Day Off* might recognize The Dream Academy songs "Please Please Please Let Me Get What I Want" and "The Edge of Forever," as snippets of those tracks are heard in that movie. *Planes, Trains and Automobiles* is another film from the 80s with a John Hughes–Dream Academy connection, featuring the band's tune "Power to Believe." Surprisingly, the very atmospheric "Life in a Northern Town" has yet to make its Hollywood debut.

Just months after "Life in a Northern Town" sprinted to #7, The Dream Academy issued a single called "The Love Parade," which reached #36 on the charts in the spring of 1986. So, the band joins the likes of Looking Glass, Nu Shooz, Swing Out Sister, and Tommy Tutone in that nebulous "Are they *really* one-hit wonders?" area. Answer: They are.

Between 1985 and their break-up in 1991, The Dream Academy waxed three albums: *The Dream Academy, Remembrance Days,* and *A Different Kind of Weather.* Their Top 10 monster was the first cut off their eponymous debut LP. "Life in a Northern Town" has also found its way onto numerous compilation CDs, including: *Just Can't Get Enough: New Wave Hits of the '80s, Vol. 15, Double Shot: Modern Rock,* and *Flashback Café, Vol. 1.* By the way, the London-based group Dario G released a track in 1998 called "Sunchyme," which was basically a dance re-mix of "Life in a Northern Town."

#16

"You Get What You Give" by New Radicals, 1999

Fashion shoots with Beck and Hanson
Courtney Love and Marilyn Manson

Peaked nationally at #36
Lead singer: Gregg Alexander
Written by Gregg Alexander and Rick Nowels

You never know where a classic one-hit single will surface: during the spring of '99, television spots for the John Cusack–Cate Blanchett movie *Pushing Tin* prominently featured "You Get What You Give," even though the song was not part of that film's soundtrack. Then, in 2002, the tune was heard on TV in New Zealand, promoting Mitsubishi's line of cars and SUVs.

New Radicals released only one album, *Maybe You've Been Brainwashed Too,* then disbanded. Of course, there really wasn't much of a *band* to *dis*band as New Radicals was essentially just singer/writer/musician Gregg Alexander. A careful inspection of the *Brainwashed* credits, however, reveals that Alexander also employed the talents of Los Angeles–based keyboard player and vocalist Danielle Brisebois, who TV viewers will remember from her acting turns on *All in the Family* and *Archie Bunker's Place.*

Gregg Alexander, who was born Gregg Aiuto, grew up in Grosse Pointe, Michigan, the tony Detroit suburb. His mother was a Jehovah's Witness, which might help explain his strangely titled song "Jehovah Made This Whole Joint for You" on the *Maybe You've Been Brainwashed Too* compact disc. By the way, before recording under the New Radicals moniker, Alexander released three albums under

his own name: *Michigan Rain, Save Me from Myself,* and *Intoxiforn-
ication*—all of which are out of print.

Part of what made "You Get What You Give" an all-time great one-
hitter was the mystery surrounding the record and its artist. New
Radicals? No one knew anything about them. Listeners were calling
stations like WPLJ, New York City's powerhouse pop/rock outlet,
completely baffled, "Hey, Jamie Lee, I have no idea who does it, don't
know the name of it either, but you gotta play that cool new tune
about kicking Marilyn Manson's ass!"

In addition, the song's meaning was appealingly inscrutable. Even
after a dozen listens, it was far from clear exactly what this manic
20-something singer was ranting about. Hope? Love? Materialism?
Karma? The message was totally up for grabs. Plus, the track's unrelenting wall of sound washed right over the entire brain, where it remained all day. The overall effect of "You Get What You Give" was
along the lines of "I'm not entirely sure what I just heard, but I can't
wait to hear it again."

It's curious that Alexander dissolved New Radicals after issuing
just one album. *Maybe You've Been Brainwashed Too's* hit single provided the FM dial with such an invigorating gust of fresh air that it
would have been interesting to see what might have come from a
sophomore effort. However, a follow-up wasn't in the cards, and
Alexander summed it up best himself: "I'd lost interest in fronting a
one-hit wonder."

Brent's Two Cents: "You Get What You Give" was easily among the
best radio hits of the late 90s, in the same league as Natalie Imbruglia's "Torn," "One Week" by Barenaked Ladies, and Smash Mouth's
"All Star."

New Radicals' "You Get What You Give," in addition to being a
wonderful record, was a highly memorable video. There was the
"band," led by an energetic Gregg Alexander, gleefully performing in
a generic shopping mall, basically causing a free-for-all. The video
poked a finger in the eye of consumerism, conformism, and every

other "ism" held dear by Middle America, and it accomplished it all with an infectious smile and good humor.

#15

"Personally" by Karla Bonoff, 1982

I can't mail it in, I can't phone it in, I can't send it in
Even by your closest kin, I'm bringing it to you per-
sonally

Peaked nationally at #19
Lead singer: Karla Bonoff
Written by Paul Kelly

Remember the Grammy-winning smash Linda Ronstadt and Aaron Neville had back in 1990 with a song called "All My Life"? Karla Bonoff wrote it. Recall tunes like "Someone to Lay Down Beside Me," "If He's Ever Near," and "Lose Again" from Ronstadt's mid-70s album *Hasten Down the Wind*? Karla Bonoff penned those also.

Ironically, Bonoff, who is recognized as among pop's best song-writers, didn't write "Personally," her lone Top 40 single. It was actually written by Paul Kelly, the respected soul singer best known for his R&B classic "Stealing in the Name of the Lord."

Although it may seem like a paradox, "Personally" creates a mood of smooth desperation. The smoothness comes primarily from Bob Glaub's deep, steady bass groove, while the desperation issues from Bonoff's vocals, which are a cry of love and lustful longing. In many ways, this record is the quintessential pop music booty call, as it positively drips with sexual desire.

"Personally" was the hit track off *Wild Heart of the Young*, Karla Bonoff's third album. The other noteworthy song from that 1982 release was "Please Be the One," a darkly beautiful tune featuring the undercurrent of a sad, slow organ throughout. "Please Be the One" actually displayed genuine chart potential, climbing to a respectable #63 before running out of gas.

When you consider that *Billboard* magazine ranked Survivor's "Eye of the Tiger" as 1982's #1 record, while "Personally" came in at #97 overall for the year, you begin to understand Bonoff's status as a one-hit wonder. The market for her brand of thoughtful, somewhat melancholy pop has always been limited. It seems like the American radio masses have historically favored rowdy, arena rock anthems over introspective, well-crafted singles. Also, by the time "Personally" charted, the musical landscape was rapidly shifting toward MTV-friendly acts like Duran Duran, Culture Club, Adam Ant, and The Fixx. These telegenic British New Wavers completely crowded out pensive singer/songwriters like Bonoff and James Taylor. Indeed, for all his tremendous commercial success, it's interesting to note that Taylor's last Top 40 hit came in early 1981, more than 20 years ago, when he landed at #11 with "Her Town Too," a duet with J.D. Souther.

Karla Bonoff remains musically active to this day, often touring with her friend Kenny Edwards. In fact, Bonoff and Edwards, along with Wendy Waldman and Andrew Gold, periodically issue albums under the name of a group called Bryndle. Andrew Gold, incidentally, is a two-hit wonder from the late 1970s, having scored with the #7 "Lonely Boy" in '77, then peaking a year later at #25 with "Thank You for Being a Friend." Bryndle member Wendy Waldman has also carved out her own spot in pop history, co-writing the Grammy-winning "Save the Best for Last," which Vanessa Williams drove all the way to #1 in 1992.

Brent's Two Cents: I've always been fascinated by the covers of Karla Bonoff's albums. Each one, without exception, presents a photo of the pretty singer facing away from the camera, her head tilted down, her eyes virtually shut. She seems so wistful, as if she's just lost her best friend. I look, in particular, at the picture featured on *Restless*

Nights and, man, I want to step right into the LP and her give a big honey-it's-going-to-be-okay hug.

#14

"Life Is a Rock (But the Radio Rolled Me)" by Reunion, 1974

Life is a rock, but the radio rolled me
Got to turn it up louder, so my DJ told me

Peaked nationally at #8
Lead singer: Joey Levine
Written by Paul DiFranco, Norman Dolph, and Joey Levine

Some have suggested that "Life Is a Rock," a quirky, surprisingly hip bubblegum tune that mentions Steely Dan, Mott the Hoople, and the Ray Charles Singers, among dozens of others, qualifies as the very first rap record, which is an intriguing thought.

"Sometimes you feel like a nut, sometimes you don't. Almond Joy's got nuts, Mounds don't." Remember that jingle from the 70s? Well, the guy who wrote it, Joey Levine, also co-wrote "Life Is a Rock (But the Radio Rolled Me)," in addition to providing the track's unforgettably rapid-fire lead vocals. "Life Is a Rock" is undoubtedly the only Top 10 single that begins with the sound of the singer taking a deep breath in preparation for the demanding work ahead.

The genius of this record lies in its simplicity—it's essentially just a recitation of the names of random rock 'n' roll acts spanning the period from the late 50s through the early 70s, all performed at breakneck speed over a chugging bass line. To some degree, and Joey Levine has been quoted as saying as much himself, "Life Is a Rock" must be credited with providing the basic blueprint and lyrical inspiration for later tunes such as Billy Joel's "We Didn't Start the Fire" and R.E.M.'s "It's the End of the World as We Know It (And I Feel Fine)."

Although this #8 smash appears on myriad compilation CDs, including *Best of Bubblegum* and *Super Hits of the '70s: Have a Nice Day, Vol. 13*, it was never released as part of a Reunion album. It's only been issued on a 45, with "Are You Ready to Believe" as its flip side.

Before Reunion, Levine enjoyed a measure of musical success as the lead singer of Ohio Express, a group that scored five Top 40 hits in the late 60s. "Yummy Yummy Yummy" was the most well known of the lot, vaulting all the way to #4 over the course of an 11-week chart run. "Yummy, yummy, yummy, I got love in my tummy, and I feel like lovin' you." Hey, it wasn't called bubblegum for nothing!

"Life Is a Rock" hit the airwaves during AM radio's last hurrah as a force in pop/rock music. By late 1974, Top 40 powerhouses like Philadelphia's WFIL, WABC and WNBC in New York, WLS and WCFL in Chicago, and KHJ in Los Angeles were losing thousands of listeners every week to the FM dial.

Brent's Two Cents: For me, "Life Is a Rock (But the Radio Rolled Me)" will forever be synonymous with doing homework in junior high school back in suburban Boston, my black Panasonic AM/FM clock radio tuned to WRKO. Harry Nelson and Johnny Dark were the RKO jocks who got me through countless hours of algebra and U.S. history. By the way, in 1979 I was a high school senior living out in the Bay Area, still doing my homework in the good company of Harry Nelson, who was then pulling the night shift on 610 KFRC in San Francisco.

Speaking of my junior high years and Boston's WRKO, here is the complete on-air lineup for that famed Top 40 station in 1974:

        6 a.m. to 9 a.m. — Dale Dorman
        9 a.m. to noon — Joel Cash
        Noon to 3 p.m. — Jack O'Brien

3 p.m. to 6 p.m.   — Harry Nelson
6 p.m. to 10 p.m. — Johnny Dark
10 p.m. to 2 a.m. — Mike Addams
2 a.m. to 6 a.m.   — J.J. Jordan

#13

"The Impression That I Get" by The Mighty Mighty Bosstones, 1997

*I've never had to knock on wood and I'm glad I
        haven't yet
Because I'm sure it isn't good, that's the impression
        that I get*

Peaked nationally at #23
Lead singer: Dicky Barrett
Written by Dicky Barrett and Joe Gittleman

On October 25, 1997, The Mighty Mighty Bosstones were the musical guests on *Saturday Night Live*. The late Chris Farley, former *SNL* cast member, hosted the program, his last-ever appearance under the lights of NBC's Studio 8-H. While most acts usually perform two songs on the show, the Bosstones performed only one tune that night, "The Impression That I Get." That year actually saw the band sing their lone Top 40 hit on national television numerous times: *Late Night with Conan O'Brien; Viva Variety,* which aired on Comedy Central; MTV's *Beach House* and *The Jenny McCarthy Show*; and *Late Show with David Letterman*.

"The Impression That I Get" was taken from the album *Let's Face It*. The Mighty Mighty Bosstones also released a live version of "Impression" on a 1998 CD called *Live from the Middle East*. In addition, the track can be found on *Ka-Boom! 16 Rockin' Tunes!*, as well as *Naked 4-Play*, compilation discs released in 1999 and 2000, respectively.

The Mighty Mighty Bosstones and Madness ("Our House" at #57) are the only ska-influenced acts on our tour of the all-time best one-hit wonders. This, of course, begs an excellent question: What exactly is ska? Well, it's a type of music that first surfaced in Jamaica back in the 60s. Ska mixed a brassy jazz sound with R&B, adding a dash of calypso for good measure. The Skatalites, Desmond Dekker, and Toots & the Maytals were among ska's most well-known pioneers. Fast forward to the late 70s and early 80s, where one finds Britishers like The Specials, The English Beat, and Madness spearheading a modestly successful ska revival, at least over in the U.K. Then, in 1997, our boys from Beantown, The Mighty Mighty Bosstones, brought ska to mainstream American radio in the form of their Top 25 single.

"The Impression That I Get" is an unusual record because it pairs happy, high energy music with serious, introspective lyrics. There is Dicky Barrett, the Bosstones' lead vocalist, baring his soul, wailing about self-doubt, all against an upbeat, party-like aural backdrop. Barrett, by the way, has acted in several movies. He played a clerk at a liquor store in 2000's *Massholes*, a film that featured stand-up comic Lenny Clarke, who starred in his own short-lived sitcom, *Lenny*, back in the early 90s. Barrett also portrayed rock 'n' roll pioneer Bill Haley in *Shake, Rattle and Roll: An American Love Story*, a television mini-series from 1999. Incidentally, all of The Mighty Mighty Bosstones appeared briefly in *Clueless*, the Alicia Silverstone flick. They, naturally enough, were cast in the role of a rock group.

Finally, The Mighty Mighty Bosstones performed at Lollapalooza '95, the alternative music festival that traveled successfully throughout the country during the 1990s. The band also contributed a song, "Zig Zag Dance," to *Elmopalooza!*, a 1998 *Sesame Street* CD. This, of course, made the Bosstones the only ska outfit with a Lollapalooza-Elmopalooza connection.

Brent's Two Cents: I always got a kick out of The Mighty Mighty Bosstones' album covers, especially *Pay Attention* and *Question the Answers*, because they sported a hip, rather primitive feel, all bright, vibrant colors and chunky, retro graphics.

#12

"Pipeline" by The Chantays, 1963

Instrumental

Peaked nationally at #4
Written by Brian Carman and Bob Spickard

"Pipeline" is the best surf instrumental of all time, with Dick Dale's "Miserlou" a close second. The Chantays' tune is also the only instrumental to rate a spot on our countdown of the greatest one-hitters.

The curious thing about the whole genre of surf music is that the tracks containing vocals, such as "Surfin' U.S.A." and "Surfer Girl" by The Beach Boys, are sunny and carefree, while the instrumentals are often decidedly dark and brooding. The mood of "Pipeline," for example, can be described as mysterious, foreboding, and even somewhat sinister—hardly what one would normally associate with a day at the beach.

The Chantays were five teenagers from Southern California's Orange County: Brian Carman, Bob Spickard, Warren Waters, Bob Marshall, and Bob Welch. Strangely, when Dot Records released "Pipeline" as a single, they misspelled the band's name as The Chantay's. When your own label can't get the group's name spelled correctly on your debut 45, that might serve as a telltale sign of a brief recording career.

Typographical errors aside, The Chantays indisputably waxed an enduring Top 40 masterpiece. Over the years, cover versions of "Pipe-

line" have been cut by artists as diverse as the late Texas bluesmaster
Stevie Ray Vaughan, Bobby "I Fought the Law" Fuller, jazz trombon-
ist Kai Winding, as well as Robert Fripp, the founder of Britain's pro-
gressive rock band King Crimson. However, the most creative cover
was done by Junior Brown on his 1996 album *Semi Crazy*, on which
he starts off with a spirited surf-meets-rockabilly treatment of "Pipeline," then drifts into the classic "Walk, Don't Run" made famous by
The Ventures, finishing with a burn-down-the-house take on Johnny
Rivers's "Secret Agent Man."

It's the deep, hypnotic bass line that most stands out upon re-
peated listenings to the original "Pipeline." The bass riff positively
sticks to the ears like glue throughout the song's entire two minutes
and twenty-two seconds.

You might be asking the obvious question: Why didn't The
Chantays enjoy another hit record? After all, they were young, energetic, and talented. Well, those familiar with the film industry adage
"If you saw the trailer, you saw the movie" have the answer. In the
case of these boys from Santa Ana, California, once you'd heard "Pipeline," you'd heard all their other tunes, too. What's more, in addition
to The Chantays, 1963 saw The Surfaris score a Top 10 hit with their
song "Wipe Out," so perhaps mainstream listeners quickly got their
fill of instrumental surf music.

Instrumental one-hit wonders have a long Top 40 history.
In 1957, for example, a saxophonist from Alabama by the
name of Bill Justis scored a #2 smash with "Raunchy," a
number that effectively alternated between a twangy electric guitar and a bluesy sax. Then, of course, there was
Bent Fabric's "Alley Cat" from 1962, the piano piece that
launched a thousand 5th-grade recitals. And, finally, who
could forget Harold Faltermeyer and his #3 record from
'85, "Axel F," which was such an integral part of the movie
Beverly Hills Cop?

The 80s and 90s, by the way, saw the emergence of bands with kitschy, colorful names like The Mermen, Laika & the Cosmonauts, Los Straitjackets, Malibooz, The Halibuts, and Aqua Velvets, all of whom were part of a so-called "surf revival," and, of course, each and every one of these groups paid homage to The Chantays by playing "Pipeline."

#11

"Come on Eileen" by Dexys Midnight Runners, 1983

Poor old Johnnie Ray
Sounded sad upon the radio

Peaked nationally at #1
Lead singer: Kevin Rowland
Written by Billy Adams, Jimmy Paterson, and
    Kevin Rowland

We've been accused of a puritanical stance towards
alcohol, again more confusion. We've got absolutely
nothing against alcohol, it just happens that we no
longer think it necessary to spend half our lives drunk,
and anyway most of us prefer tea.
            —Excerpt from an insert included with the
            single "Show Me"

This unforgettable tune opens with a lazy, dreamy fiddle right out of County Cork, then immediately shifts into foot-stomping pop overdrive. Easily one of the most hum-able, gets-stuck-in-your-brain singles of the 80s, "Come on Eileen" went straight to the top of the American charts in 1983. The record also held down the #1 spot in the U.K. Because of the track's distinct Celtic flavor, many listeners assumed Dexys Midnight Runners were an Irish band, but they actually hailed from Birmingham, England. While Dexys underwent numerous personnel changes throughout their eight-year history, the line-up at the time of their lone U.S. success was Billy Adams, Micky Billingham, Giorgio Kilkenny, Brian Maurice, Jimmy Paterson, Kevin Rowland, Seb Shelton, and Paul Speare, with Rowland serving as the leader.

"Come on Eileen" was from the album *Too-Rye-Ay*. The song also surfaced on the *Tommy Boy* soundtrack, the Chris Farley–David Spade film. In the late 90s, Save Ferris, a band out of Southern California, released an album called *It Means Everything*, on which they covered "Come on Eileen."

Interestingly, from its inception way back in July of 1978 through its break-up in 1986, the proper spelling of the first word of this group's name was always clouded in confusion, especially among the press. Was it *Dexy's* with an apostrophe or *Dexys* sans apostrophe? For example, a 1980 *Record Mirror* magazine review of an early tune called "Geno" had it as Dexy's. However, a year later, the very same *Record Mirror* printed an open letter from the band to the publication's readership. This letter was signed Dexys Midnight Runners— *no* apostrophe. The bottom line is that going by no less of an authority than the band's album covers, it's plain to see that the correct spelling was *without* an apostrophe, although to this day you'll consistently see it misspelled as Dexy's. Incidentally, even though frontman Kevin Rowland has remained cagey concerning the subject over the years, it's widely held that Dexys Midnight Runners took their name from the amphetamine Dexedrine.

On May 14, 1983, Dexys Midnight Runners sang "Come on Eileen" on NBC's *Saturday Night Live*. Ed Koch, then mayor of New York City, hosted that evening. During that same period, the spring of '83, which proved to be the height of the Runners' popularity, it was seemingly impossible to turn on MTV for more than 20 minutes without catching a glimpse of the "Eileen" video. There was a scruffy, skinny Kevin Rowland clad in blue overalls and bandana, singing and hopping around a generic working-class British neighborhood, his mates in tow.

By the way, the "poor old Johnnie Ray" in the first line of the tune is a nod to an American singer who enjoyed tremendous popularity in England throughout the 1950s. Johnnie Ray was known for his highly wrought, break-out-the-hankies torch songs.

Modern bluesman Peter Malick wrote a song "Eileen (If You Only Knew)." An outfit from Pittsburgh called Ploughman's Lunch recorded an original track entitled simply "Eileen." But only Dexys Midnight Runners, a spirited band of ragamuffins from the north of England, ever carried the name Eileen to the very heights of the American charts.

#10

"Get Here" by Oleta Adams, 1991

You can reach me by caravan, cross the desert like an
Arab man
I don't care how you get here, just get here if you can

Peaked nationally at #5
Lead singer: Oleta Adams
Written by Brenda Russell

In 1988, Brenda Russell released an album called *Get Here*, the title track of which failed to chart. Two years later, Oleta Adams issued *Circle of One*, her debut album, which also included "Get Here." By early '91, Adams's cover version of that Russell-penned tune had shot to #5.

Why did Oleta Adams's re-make become a Top 10 smash, while Brenda Russell's original couldn't even dent the upper reaches of the Top 40? The short answer to that question is a single word: timing.

The release of Adams's rendition coincided with a nervous America's entry into the Persian Gulf War, and the families of U.S. servicemen and -women quickly adopted "Get Here" as their theme song. With feelings of patriotism running high, Oleta Adams's powerful voice blanketed the nation's airwaves, expressing the fervent hope of millions for the safe, speedy return home of our troops: "I don't care how you get here, just get here if you can. . . ."

Of course, patriotism can carry a song only so far, so it didn't hurt "Get Here's" fortunes that Adams brought a polished, soulful set of pipes to the effort. The way she starts off slowly, almost methodically, never rushes things and allows the track to naturally develop a full head of steam is a delight to experience as a listener.

Before the success of "Get Here," Oleta Adams was best known for her work with the British group Tears for Fears, turning in a memorable performance on the song "Woman in Chains." Today, the singer resides in Kansas City, Kansas, from where she continues to make albums and pursue an active touring schedule.

By the way, Patti LuPone, Barbara Mandrell, and Livingston Taylor, younger brother of James Taylor, have all covered "Get Here." An instrumental version is also found on *Saxophone Dreams*, a CD from the year 2000.

Brent's Two Cents: Brenda Russell, the aforementioned writer of Oleta Adams's hit "Get Here," is, for her own part, a two-hit wonder, scoring a #30 record in 1979 with "So Good, So Right," followed almost a decade later by the #6 single "Piano in the Dark" in the spring of '88. I still hear "Piano" spun occasionally on CD-101, the smooth jazz station in New York City. As for "So Good, So Right," a tune I remember receiving modest radio play in Southern California when I was a freshman at UCLA, it has unfortunately faded into radio oblivion. You never hear this track anymore on the Big Apple's airwaves, which is a shame because it would be a natural addition to an Oldies station's playlist, like WBCS-FM or even Lite-FM WLTW.

Speaking of two-hit wonders such as Brenda Russell, other memorable artists with exactly two Top 40 charters to their credit include: Carl Carlton, "Everlasting Love" (#6 in 1974) and "She's a Bad Mama Jama (She's Built, She's Stacked)" (#22 in 1981); Blue Oyster Cult, "(Don't Fear) The Reaper" (#12 in 1976) and "Burnin' for You" (#40 in 1981); and Leon Russell "Tight Rope" (#11 in 1972) and "Lady Blue" (#14 in 1975).

#9

"Mary's Prayer" by Danny Wilson, 1987

Save me, save me, be the light in my eyes
What I wouldn't give to be when I was Mary's prayer

Peaked nationally at #23
Lead singer: Gary Clark
Written by Gary Clark

Often called Scotland's answer to Steely Dan, Danny Wilson flashed across the pop sky during the late 1980s. Unlike Steely Dan, though, this trio composed of brothers Gary and Kit Clark along with Gerard "Ged" Grimes scored only one hit record, "Mary's Prayer," which reached #23 in the summer of '87.

Danny Wilson took their name from *Meet Danny Wilson*, a little-remembered black and white film from 1952 starring Frank Sinatra, Shelley Winters, and Raymond Burr. In fact, the group's debut album, on which "Mary's Prayer" appears, was called simply *Meet Danny Wilson*.

Two things make Danny Wilson's lone Top 40 single shine as an all-time great one-hitter: Gary Clark's energetic vocals and Ged Grimes's muscular bass line. Clark's voice has this unusual Billy-Joel-with-a-Scottish-lilt quality to it that is extremely appealing. He approaches

"Mary's Prayer" with a smooth urgency, reminiscent of Joel's performance in "Only the Good Die Young." As for Grimes's bass playing, it's notable for the way it propels the track forward. He isn't just noodling away in the background, he's pushing the song ahead with a deep, insistent groove.

At the time of "Mary's Prayer's" radio run in 1987, an English band called Swing Out Sister was also enjoying success with a jazzy Top 10 track called "Breakout," and for a spell, it seemed as if stylish, intelligent pop was poised to carve a solid niche on the charts. This, of course, never happened. By '88, Danny Wilson had completely vanished from the musical radar. As for Swing Out Sister, they followed up "Breakout" with "Twilight World," a minor hit topping out at #31. That group then dropped totally off the map. Apparently, the mainstream's appetite for this brand of urbane, polished pop was quickly satisfied, which explains Danny Wilson's status as a one-hit wonder.

During Danny Wilson's brief existence, 1987 through 1990, they produced two albums of original material—the aforementioned *Meet Danny Wilson* and 1989's *Bebop Moptop*. While their second album failed to spawn any hit singles, it did contain a tune called "Ballad of Me and Shirley MacLaine," which has to be counted among the goofier, self-conscious song titles of the 80s.

Today, all three former members of Danny Wilson continue making music. Kit Clark fronts the five-piece, wryly named outfit Swiss Family Orbison, while his brother, Gary, has been involved with a band called Transister, in addition to pursuing a solo recording career, often with the help of his old bandmate Ged Grimes.

By the way, Cameron Diaz and Ben Stiller fans will recall "Mary's Prayer" from *There's Something About Mary*, the late 90s Bobby and Peter Farrelly comedy. Danny Wilson's hit shares that movie's soundtrack with such pop classics as "Build Me Up Buttercup" by The Foundations and "Is She Really Going Out With Him?" by Joe "Look Sharp!" Jackson. And, seeing how the band originated in the city of Dundee, hard by the north bank of the River Tay, it's only fitting that

"Mary's Prayer" is also found on a compilation CD called *Best Scottish Album in the World Ever*.

Brent's Two Cents: Danny Wilson's "Mary's Prayer," "Breakout" by Swing Out Sister, Gregory Abbott's "Shake You Down," and "Keep Your Hands to Yourself" by The Georgia Satellites were among the most memorable singles of 1987. It pleases me to no end that these four terrific songs were all released by one-hit wonders.

#8

"Smoke from a Distant Fire" by The Sanford/Townsend Band, 1977

If things are the same then explain why your kiss is
*   so cold*
And that mist in your eyes feels like rain on the fire
*   in my soul*

Peaked nationally at #9
Lead singer: John Townsend
Written by Ed Sanford, John Townsend, and
       Steven Stewart

"Smoke from a Distant Fire" was that rare record that just flat-out cooked from the first note to the very last. It boasted a swinging, brassy bar-band sound that made you want to take a good, healthy swig of your longneck Bud and get out on the dance floor. However, popular taste in music changes rapidly, and just three or four years later, songs like this had completely vanished from the Top 40, crowded off the radio dial by the arrival of New Wave and synth pop. Hello, Human League. Good-bye, Sanford/Townsend.

   The group released three albums: *Smoke from a Distant Fire* (on which Kenny Loggins can be heard singing backup vocals), *Duo-Glide* (1977), and *Nail Me to the Wall* (1979), none of which remains in print in the United States; interestingly, though, Sanford/Townsend's first two LPs were re-released on a Japanese label in 2000. However, the single "Smoke from a Distant Fire" is readily available on compilation CDs such as *Super Hits of the '70s: Have a Nice Day, Vol. 20* and *Rock On 1977*, where it's sandwiched between Mary MacGregor's "Torn Between Two Lovers" and "Year of the Cat" by Al Stewart.

The year 1977 looked rather favorably, and some might even say charitably, upon one-hit wonders: David Soul reached #1 with "Don't Give Up On Us," "Undercover Angel" shot Alan O'Day to the top spot, and of course, Debby Boone scored a multi-week *numero uno* smash with "You Light Up My Life." Other one-hitters from '77 included Floaters, who peaked at #2 with "Float On," and Paul "Heaven on the 7th Floor" Nicholas. In this wimpy, treacly pop climate, it's surprising that a spirited song like "Smoke from a Distant Fire" managed to crack the Top 10. It could be, though, that a single displaying some genuine rock 'n' roll heart was precisely the tonic needed to revitalize such a decidely bland musical period.

Messrs. Sanford and Townsend are remembered today as quintessential 70s one-hitters due in large measure to lousy timing. They arrived on the chart scene probably about five years too late to be properly appreciated. If "Smoke from a Distant Fire" had come out circa '72 or '73, the track would have meshed beautifully with the likes of, say, The Doobie Brothers' "China Grove" or "A Horse with No Name" by America. So, by the time "Black Water" and "Sister Golden Hair" were charting in 1975, The Sanford/Townsend Band would have been fully along for the ride, most likely resting comfortably on at least three hit singles. However, when your first tune breaks in 1977, it's a whole different ballgame. All of a sudden, you're trying to navigate Top 40 waters clogged with disco divas and disco ducks, not to mention Bay City Rollers. Needless to say, if you're an outfit selling a brand of pop with a slightly smoky, three-day-growth edge, the Jimmy Carter era might not have provided the most fertile musical soil in which to flourish.

After The Sanford/Townsend Band called it a day in 1979, Ed Sanford and John Townsend continued working in the entertainment business. Sanford contributed music to the 1987 action flick *Let's Get Harry*, which starred Mark Harmon and Robert Duvall. As for Townsend, he issued an enthusiastically received solo album in early 2003 called *The Road Leads Home*.

#7

"I Love You Always Forever" by Donna Lewis, 1996

I love you always forever
Near and far closer together

Peaked nationally at #2
Lead singer: Donna Lewis
Written by Kevin Killen and Donna Lewis

"Proud Mary" #2. "Bad Moon Rising" #2. "Green River" #2. "Travelin' Band" #2. "Lookin' Out My Back Door" #2. On five separate occasions during the late 60s and early 70s, Credence Clearwater Revival, the California swamp-rockers led by John Fogerty, were frustrated in their quest for a chart-topping single, each time stalling just before the finish line. Donna Lewis must have known how C.C.R. felt when, back in the summer of 1996, her song "I Love You Always Forever" remained stuck at #2 for more than two months, being denied the top spot by "Macarena (Bayside Boys Mix)," which the one-hitters Los del Rio planted at #1 for an astonishing 14 weeks. The Welsh-born singer kept banging on the door, the duo from Spain stubbornly refused to answer.

Even though "I Love You Always Forever" failed to reach pop's pinnacle, according to the radio station monitoring firm Broadcast Data Systems, it holds the distinction of being the first record ever heard over a seven-day period by a cumulative American radio audience in excess of 100 million listeners. This remarkable fact should come as no surprise, however, when you realize Lewis's smash spent an almost-unheard-of nine months in the Top 40. Consider that Celine Dion's "Because You Loved Me," another monster tune from the mid-90s, logged five *fewer* weeks on the charts, and you get a sense of just how enormously successful "I Love You Always Forever" actually was.

As Lewis began her marathon radio run, some in the music press dismissed her record's sound, knocking it for being "too slick" and "overproduced." The critics, however, badly misjudged the public's musical taste. In fact, ASCAP (The American Society of Composers, Authors and Publishers) determined that "I Love You Always Forever" was among the most played songs, if not *the* most played, for the three-year period from 1996 through 1998.

"I Love You Always Forever" is cleverly constructed. The track begins languorously, Lewis's vocals drifting like a wispy cloud, then, just as somnolence is about to take hold, a pulsating beat kicks in with an unrelenting *clickety-clack, clickety-clack, clickety-clack,* steering the song in a completely different, energetic direction.

Today, this Lewis tune has become a wedding reception staple, right up there with Joshua Kadison's "Beautiful in My Eyes" and "(Everything I Do) I Do It for You" by Bryan Adams, who, by the way, has charted a hard-to-fathom 22 times. Incidentally, covers of "I Love You Always Forever" and "(Everything I Do) I Do It for You" appear on the K-Tel CD *The Wedding Collection*, which might be the only musical compilation to ever spotlight "Ave Maria" and "Here Comes the Bride," in addition to "The Hokey Pokey" and "Mambo No. 5."

Donna Lewis was born in Wales, a corner of the U.K. that also spawned one-hitters Shirley Bassey and Scritti Politti. Bassey, of course, enjoyed the #5 "Goldfinger" back in 1965, while the oddly named band Scritti Politti hit chart paydirt in '85 with "Perfect Way." Spencer Davis, Badfinger, David Gray, Mary "Those Were the Days" Hopkin, John Cale, Dave Edmunds, and, needless to say, Tom Jones are other famous pop/rock acts with strong Welsh ties.

Brent's Two Cents: Considering what a Top 40 juggernaut Lewis had with "I Love You Always Forever," it's a genuine shock to me that she never scored a follow-up hit. Mind you, the singer has sold millions of records worldwide, and has undoubtedly done very well for herself, but it's still puzzling why she remains a one-hit wonder. The enormous buzz and momentum she created with her wildly successful 1996 debut single surely should have carried over to at least one or two more chart toppers by the end of the 90s. Never happened, though.

#6

"True" by Spandau Ballet, 1983

Take your seaside arms and write the next line
Oh, I want the truth to be known

Peaked nationally at #4
Lead singer: Tony Hadley
Written by Gary Kemp

"Take your seaside arms and write the next line..." One question springs immediately to mind: What, exactly, are "seaside arms"? Must be a British thing.

The next time the Molly Ringwald flick *Sixteen Candles* airs on a rainy Saturday afternoon, pay close attention during the high school dance scene and you'll hear "True" playing softly in the background. This early 80s track can definitely stake a legitimate claim as the quintessential slow groove, teenage makeout song. "True" can also be heard at the very end of the Adam Sandler–Drew Barrymore movie *The Wedding Singer*.

This record's success rests mainly on Tony Hadley's smooth, confident lead vocals. His voice, which blends beautifully with the lush, dreamy background harmonies, exudes a cool, somewhat plaintive sexiness. The record is also memorable for Steve Norman's extended sax solo, a 37-second jazzy riff that elegantly bridges the tune's middle to its end.

Spandau Ballet was composed of brothers Gary and Martin Kemp, Tony Hadley, Steve Norman, and John Keeble. Film fans will remember the Kemps from their starring roles in *The Krays*, a 1990 British production about Reginald and Ronald Kray, the notorious gangster twins from 1960s London. By the way, *The Krays* featured one of the most ominous taglines in cinematic history: *When people are afraid of you, you can do anything. Remember that.* Do you suppose Martin Kemp ever used those lines on the Culture Club's Boy George?

Gary and Martin Kemp always viewed themselves more as actors than musicians, which contributed to Spandau Ballet's demise in the early 90s. After leaving the band, Gary appeared in movies such as *The Bodyguard* (he was Whitney Houston's publicist) and *Killing Zoe*, a French film starring Eric Stoltz. He also landed a role in a 1993 episode of *The Larry Sanders Show*, the Gary Shandling vehicle on HBO. As for younger brother Martin, during the late 80s and on through the 90s, he was seen on television in *Highlander, The Outer Limits,* and *Tales from the Crypt.* He also played the Steve Owen character on the popular British TV program *EastEnders*.

Tony Hadley, for his part, continues to make records as a solo artist. In fact, in 1997 he released a critically acclaimed self-titled album on which he covered songs by Duran Duran ("Save a Prayer"), Hall & Oates ("She's Gone"), Tom Petty ("Free Fallin'"), and Tears for Fears

("Woman in Chains"). Interestingly, Oleta Adams, who is ranked #10 on our list of one-hitters on the strength of her 1991 smash "Get Here," sang on the original Tears for Fears version of "Woman in Chains."

By the way, according to Gary Kemp, it was his friend, Bob Elms, who gave the band its peculiar name. Elms had visited a rock club in Germany, where he noticed the graffito *Spandau Ballet* scrawled on the men's room wall. The phrase stuck with him, and he suggested it to Kemp as the perfect moniker. Spandau, incidentally, is a district in Berlin, site of the infamous Spandau Prison, which housed Nazi war criminals after World War II, most notably Hitler's deputy Rudolph Hess. That an English group strongly identified with the fashion-conscious New Romantic movement of the early 80s would choose to associate itself with a notorious German jailhouse is just another example of pop music's affinity for the ironic.

Brent's Two Cents: Yes, I'm fully aware of the band's other two Top 40 singles: "Gold," which reached #29 and "Only When You Leave," a #34 record. With respect to the latter "hit," it goes without saying that nobody, apart from perhaps three giggly teenage girls in Tokyo who've put up a Spandau Ballet tribute site on the Internet, has even the foggiest recollection of "Only When You Leave." As for "Gold," I certainly remember hearing this tune a half-dozen times on the radio, but when your debut song rockets to #4, your follow-up release just plain must do better than a pedestrian #29 on the charts, otherwise you remain a one-hitter. This much is true.

#5

"I Touch Myself" by Divinyls, 1991

I don't want anybody else
When I think about you, I touch myself

Peaked nationally at #4
Lead singer: Christina Amphlett
Written by Tom Kelly, Mark McEntee, William Steinberg,
    and Christina Amphlett

It's ["I Touch Myself"] one of those songs that can be
taken on different levels. And I think it's up to the
listener's interpretation of that song—if you're a nun,
you know, you're going to interpret it in one way, and if
you're a stripper, you're going to interpret it in another,
you know.

—CHRISTINA AMPHLETT, AS QUOTED IN
ILLINOIS ENTERTAINER

For millions of randy teenage boys, "I Touch Myself," the Divinyls' #4
smash from 1991, was, in many ways, the original VH-1 pop-up video.
There was lead singer/vixen Christina Amphlett slithering around in
her slinky black mini-skirt and above-the-knee black boots. The whole
effect was similar to Cher's provocative, *damn-it-feels-wonderful-to-*
be-half-naked-on-the-deck-of-a-battleship performance in her "If I
Could Turn Back Time" video. And notwithstanding Amphlett's "it's up
to the listener's interpretation" statement above, the Divinyls' Top 5
record was, in fact, deliciously unambiguous in its meaning. From the
very first spin, everyone knew the tune was plainly and unapologeti-
cally about female masturbation. Cyndi Lauper's "She Bop" and "I
Touch Myself"—well, the Eurythmics and Aretha Franklin put it best
in late 1985 when they sang "Sisters Are Doin' It for Themselves."

The Divinyls, who formed in Sydney, Australia, in the early 1980s, are essentially the duo of Christina Amphlett and Mark McEntee. To date, the outfit has released nine albums, their debut being 1983's *Desperate*, the most recent, *Live* from 2001. While extremely famous Down Under, Ms. Amphlett and Mr. McEntee are the prototypical 90s American one-hit wonders. Mind you, the group did land a #76 single in the mid-80s with "Pleasure and Pain," but the musical equation remains quite simple: Divinyls = "I Touch Myself."

"I Touch Myself" was included on the *Austin Powers: International Man of Mystery* soundtrack. The Divinyls' lone hit was also featured in *Prelude to a Kiss*, a 1992 movie starring Meg Ryan and Alec Baldwin. In addition, Amphlett and McEntee can be heard doing a number called "Ain't Gonna Eat My Heart Out Anymore" on the *Buffy the Vampire Slayer* CD. And, speaking of the silver screen, Christina Amphlett made her acting debut in an obscure 1982 film called *Monkey Grip*. The Divinyls also contributed to the *Monkey Grip* soundtrack. Incidentally, in the late 90s, Amphlett did a critically praised turn on the Sydney stage as Judy Garland in a musical called *The Boy from Oz*, which told the story of the late Australian entertainer Peter Allen.

Today, the names Christina Amphlett and Mark McEntee are largely forgotten here in the United States, but in the spring of 1991, the Divinyls made the long journey from Down Under, carrying with them a sexy, flirtatious song called "I Touch Myself," an all-time classic one-hit single.

Other Aussie one-hitters include Midnight Oil, who scored a #17 hit with "Beds Are Burning" in the summer of 1988, The Church, a Canberra-based outfit that landed at #24 in '88 with "Under the Milky Way," as well as Rolf Harris, who climbed all the way to #3 in 1963 with the silly ditty "Tie Me Kangaroo Down, Sport." Two other Australian acts, Air Supply and Rick Springfield, regrettably were not one-hit wonders.

#4

"Beach Baby" by The First Class, 1974

Do you remember back in old L.A.—oh, oh, oh
When everybody drove a Chevrolet—oh, oh, oh

Peaked nationally at #4
Lead singer: Tony Burrows
Written by John Carter and Gillian Shakespeare

Elton [John] used to be a session singer, as well. We
used to work together many years ago. He was called
Reg Dwight then.

> —TONY BURROWS, AS QUOTED ON PMP
> NETWORK, PMPNETWORK.COM

The story of "Beach Baby" and The First Class is really the fascinating tale of Englishman Tony Burrows, a guy who has sometimes been referred to as "The Greatest Pop Singer Whose Name You've Never Heard." Like fellow Brit Paul Carrack (the lead vocalist of Ace, #42 on our tour of pop's best one-hitters), Tony Burrows is living proof that, curiously, one can be famous to several generations of music lovers on both sides of the Atlantic and yet remain totally unknown at the same time.

Millions of baby boomers will fondly remember the following Top 40 tunes coming out of their futuristic-looking Panasonic AM/FM clock radios in the early and mid-70s:

"Love Grows (Where My Rosemary Goes)" by Edison
      Lighthouse
"My Baby Loves Lovin'" by White Plains
"United We Stand" by Brotherhood of Man
"Gimme Dat Ding" by The Pipkins

And, of course, "Beach Baby" by The First Class. Five one-hit wonders by five different bands. Amazingly, our man Tony Burrows sang lead vocals on each of those tracks.

The most impressive thing about a thoroughly English studio group like The First Class is that they had the musical talent to successfully pull off such a quintessential California sun-and-surf record as "Beach Baby." Can't you just picture Burrows and the other session guys sitting in the studio on a typical drizzly, dreary London day singing joyously about Chevrolets and San Jose!

What earns "Beach Baby" a spot among the all-time greatest one-hit wonders is the unusual way it marries that distinctive 70s AM pop style with a Phil Spector–ish sound. It's British Bubblegum meets the American Wall of Sound. This is a fun, timeless single that sounds as fresh today as it did back in '74. By the way, "Beach Baby" was originally issued on The First Class's eponymous debut album, and, naturally, over the years, the #4 smash has also found its way onto a variety of compilation CDs, including: *Have A Nice Decade: The '70s*

Tony Burrows and The First Class will forever be associated with a sub-genre of pop called bubblegum, a brand of music that has too often been unfairly disparaged. We can start with excellent, enduring one-hit singles featuring Burrows like "Beach Baby" and "Love Grows (Where My Rosemary Goes)" and head straight on down the line with a whole stack of fun, memorable records that all fall under the bubblegum banner: "Billy, Don't Be a Hero" and "Who Do You Think You Are" by Bo Donaldson and The Heywoods; "The Night Chicago Died" by Paper Lace; "Life Is a Rock (But the Radio Rolled Me)" by Reunion; "Heartbeat (It's a Love Beat)" by The DeFranco Family; "Little Willy" and "Ballroom Blitz" by Sweet; and "The Rain, the Park and Other Things" by The Cowsills.

Pop Culture Box, The Best Summer Album in the World—Ever, and *Forever Gold: British Invasion.*

We end with two more pieces of cool Tony Burrows trivia: First, as part of an early 60s band called The Kestrels, he toured with The Beatles. Second, the ubiquitous "I'd like to buy the world a Coke" television commercials from the 1970s, well, Burrows's voice can be heard on those spots, too. Not bad for a one-hit wonder—or, should we more accurately say, a *five*-hit wonder.

#3

"Into the Night" by Benny Mardones, 1980

If I could fly, I'd pick you up
I'd take you into the night

Peaked nationally at #11
Lead singer: Benny Mardones
Written by Robert Tepper and Benny Mardones

You might be surprised to learn that, according to The American Society of Composers, Authors and Publishers (ASCAP), one-hitter Benny Mardones has managed to get his song "Into the Night" spun over the airwaves in excess of four million times. To put this in perspective, ASCAP estimates that "Yesterday," the famous Beatles tune, has been aired on American radio some 10 million times, making it the most played single in history. So, while nobody will ever mistake Mardones for Lennon and McCartney, the fact is that "Into the Night" now ranks in the Top 25 in terms of all-time national airplay.

"Into the Night" actually charted twice in the same decade, reaching #11 in 1980, then nine years later landing at #20. Indeed, apart from a perennial holiday record like Bing Crosby's "White Christmas," what Mardones accomplished in terms of hitting chart paydirt more than once with the exact same single is virtually unheard of. Radio lore has it that in early '89, nearly ten years after its initial release, KZZP-FM in Phoenix decided to put "Into the Night" back into its rotation, based on an enthusiastic, and completely unexpected, reaction to Mardones's name being raised on a "Where are they now?" feature. Listeners in Arizona ate it up, sparking a brief Benny Mardones revival nationwide.

When his song broke into the Top 40 for the second time, the Cleveland native, who boasted an impressive three-and-a-half-octave vocal range, was living in Paris, of all places, *without* a record contract. What's more, *Never Run, Never Hide*, the album on which "Into the Night" appeared, was long out of print. Not surprisingly, upon learning of the renewed interest in his 1980 track, Mardones returned to the United States from France in hopes of capitalizing on the unusual circumstances. Arriving back in America, he cut an album, *Benny Mardones*, which featured an updated "Into the Night." It's interesting to note, however, that this new version was not the one DJs were spinning in '89, choosing instead to stick with the original.

Today, "Into the Night" is available on any number of compilation CDs, including *Retro Lunchbox: Gooey Love Songs, Radio Daze: Pop Hits of the '80s, Vol. 3*, and *No. 1 Hits of the 80's*, where it appears alongside "Pilot of the Airwaves" by one-hitter Charlie Dore. Of course, Dore's song peaked at #13, Mardones's at #11, but apparently that's close enough to be considered a "No. 1 Hit" by the generous-of-chart-spirit folks over at the Rebound label.

As mentioned earlier, "Into the Night" is that rarest of pop songs in that it managed two distinct Top 40 runs. Was this just plain dumb luck because some program director in Phoenix decided to act on a hunch? Perhaps, but the explanation probably goes deeper. "Into the Night" is one of those uncommon numbers that doesn't seem to belong to any particular era or genre. You hear, for example, "Cars" by one-hitter Gary Numan and it positively screams early 80s New Wave.

Not so with the Benny Mardones record. It just as easily could have been initially released in the 60s, 70s, 80s, or 90s—its sound is that hard to pin down and timeless.

Benny Mardones remains the prototypical one-hit wonder, the proverbial flash-in-the-pan: the singer who enjoys a moment in the Top 40 limelight, then quickly fades into oblivion. These days, Mardones resides in Los Angeles, where he's still making music, occasionally playing live gigs with his band, Benny Mardones & The Hurricanes. He's still searching for that elusive second hit record—or, who knows, maybe a third chart go with "Into the Night."

#2

"Stay"
by Maurice Williams & The Zodiacs, 1960

Stay! Aaahhh . . .
Just a little bit longer

Peaked nationally at #1
Lead singer: Maurice Williams
Written by Maurice Williams

If you ever come across an old 45 r.p.m. single that was pressed specifically for use by a commercial radio station, you'll notice that in addition to listing the song's total length, the label will probably also give the duration of the track's instrumental introduction. This was important information during the heyday of AM Top 40 because it let the DJ know exactly how many seconds he had for his patter before the vocal portion of the record kicked in. So, a label might read something like INTRO. :17 or INTRO. :08. Occasionally, though, a disk jockey would see this: INTRO. COLD, which meant the song contained no introduction at all—basically, spin the platter and get out of the way.

Lita Ford's "Kiss Me Deadly," "Mary's Prayer" by the Scottish band Danny Wilson, and "Stay" are three classic one-hitters known for their *cold intros*. After dropping the needle on Maurice Williams's #1 smash, the very first thing you hear is The Zodiacs shouting "Stay!"

Clocking in at a brisk 95 seconds, "Stay" is the shortest one-hit wonder on our list. Indeed, it's among the shortest records to *ever* crack the charts. Incidentally, the "Stay" 45 was first issued on Herald Records, Al Silver's pioneering label noted for bringing black R&B acts to the attention of mainstream white audiences.

The most remarkable thing about this song is its timeless quality. Written in the early 50s, recorded in 1960, later heard on the 1978 *American Hot Wax* soundtrack, then featured in the Jennifer Grey–Patrick Swayze movie *Dirty Dancing* from 1987, the tune glides agelessly from decade to decade. One can easily imagine people shaking their bones to "Stay" 50 years from now, as it's that much of a pop music evergreen.

Also notable is just how many times "Stay" has been successfully covered since its initial release. Jackson Browne hit #20 with his 1978 version, while The Four Seasons rode their rendition to #16 in the spring of '64. Rufus (featuring Chaka Khan) reached the #38 spot with his cover in the late 70s, and, although not landing in the Top 40, other artists recording "Stay" included Lou Christie and The Hollies. Jackson Browne's cover, by the way, is particularly memorable for the wonderful falsetto singing of David Lindley, a fitting tribute to Shane Gaston's high-pitched work on the original.

It's difficult to explain precisely why Maurice Williams & The Zodiacs failed to score a second hit single. Their timing was certainly good—apart from Elvis, the very early 60s saw few, if any, acts dominating the charts, and with the British Invasion still several years away, the group didn't find itself facing especially stiff musical competition during that period. Of course, over the past 40-plus years, "Stay" alone has sold, by some estimates, more than 10 million copies worldwide, which obviously goes a long way toward salving any hurt Maurice Williams may have experienced in chasing that elusive follow-up hit record.

Approaching the age of 65 and making his home in Charlotte, North Carolina, Maurice Williams shows few signs of slowing down, as he continues performing dozens of live shows every year, primarily in the Southeast. As for recording, as recently as 2000, Maurice Williams & The Zodiacs (interestingly, the group was originally dubbed Maurice Williams & The Gladiolas) released an album called *Back to Basics*, which, somewhat surprisingly, included the Bob Seger–written "Against the Wind." Coming as no surprise, however, was the CD's second track—the indefatigable "Stay."

#1

"Walking in Memphis"
by Marc Cohn, 1991

And she said, "Tell me, are you a Christian, child?"
And I said, "Ma'am, I am tonight"

Peaked nationally at #13
Lead singer: Marc Cohn
Written by Marc Cohn

Inspiring, heartfelt lyrics that tell a vivid story of loneliness, exploration, and hope, all set against music that is, by turns, sad and uplifting. In four minutes, "Walking in Memphis" succeeds beautifully in expressing what it's like to be alive in this crazy, wonderful world—the fear, frustration, and isolation, but also the joy, wonderment, and sense of community.

When you combine an unusually insightful lyrical message with superb vocals, and then blend that together with rich, evocative musical accompaniment, the result is an extremely special song, a record that really stands out from the crowd, which is why Marc Cohn and his "Walking in Memphis" earns the top spot on our tour of the all-time best one-hit wonders.

It's been called the "Curse of the Grammy." And, if you examine the facts, it's hard to argue the point: Best New Artist 1976: The Starland Vocal Band; Best New Artist 1980: Christopher Cross; Best New Artist 1989: Milli Vanilli; Best New Artist 1992: Arrested Development. You get the picture. So, when he heard the words: "And the 1991 Grammy for Best New Artist goes to . . . Marc Cohn!"—well, let's just say this talented Cleveland-born singer and songwriter should have made an immediate beeline for the exit rather than join that group of previous "winners."

On July 19, 1986, Caroline Kennedy, the only daughter of John F. Kennedy and Jacqueline Kennedy Onassis, married Edwin Schlossberg. A 27-year-old Marc Cohn fronted the wedding band that played on that summer's day. Five years later, on the strength of his Top 20 smash, "Walking in Memphis," Cohn took home the jinxed Grammy for Best New Artist. Michael Bolton won the Grammy that year for Best Pop Vocal Performance by a Male for his work on "When a Man Loves a Woman," proving once more that there is no musical justice.

Cher covered "Walking in Memphis" on her *It's a Man's World* album, which she released in 1996. That same year, John Tesh recorded an instrumental version of Cohn's hit. Both covers paled in comparison to the original. By the way, a song called "True Companion," which was on the same album as "Walking in Memphis," occasionally finds airtime on Lite-FM stations; however, "True Companion" never reached the Top 40. To this day, "Walking in Memphis" remains Marc Cohn's signature (and only) hit single.

During the late 90s, Cohn could be heard singing "you make the world taste better" on TV spots for Dr Pepper. Going into the new millennium, Marc Cohn has been pursuing an active touring schedule, performing at a diverse range of venues, including Bimbo's 365 Club in San Francisco; New York's Carnegie Hall; The Washington Zoo in the nation's capital; and the Meadowbrook Farm Musical Arts Center in Gilford, New Hampshire.

Conclusion

We started our tour of the all-time best one-hit wonders with "Walking on Sunshine" by Katrina & the Waves, and we ended with "Walking in Memphis" by Marc Cohn. And what a terrific walk through pop music it's been!

Although we covered a lot of ground, there were, naturally, many excellent acts who, primarily because of their relative obscurity, were not written about. So, let's give a nod to the following lesser-known one-hit wonders: Roseanne Cash ("Seven Year Ache"); The Crusaders ("Street Life"); David & David ("Welcome to the Boomtown"); Gunhill Road ("Back When My Hair Was Short"); McGuinn, Clark & Hillman ("Don't You Write Her Off"); Moving Pictures ("What About Me"); Benjamin Orr ("Stay the Night"); Siouxsie & The Banshees ("Kiss Them for Me"); Smokie ("Living Next Door to Alice"); and Roger Voudouris ("Get Used to It").

About the Author

Brent Mann is a writer living in New York City. *99 Red Balloons* is his first book. You can visit Brent on the Web at www.brentmann.com.